# Testimonials

"We purchased Mr. Durrett's Senior Cohousing Handbook about a year ago and it is our most dog-eared resource. We read it first for general information and return to it again and again as we are ready for deeper understanding."
— Sheila, Prince Edward Island Senior Cohousing

"Thank you a million times for starting this project and inspiring us with the confidence that we could make it happen. If it weren't for you this special place would not exist." — Taryn, Vancouver Cohousing, Vancouver, British Columbia

"The Cohousing Company [McCamant & Durrett Architects] rescued us. Within a month, our conflicts and frustrations were transformed into creative challenge and our group coalesced into an energized and cohesive community."
— Brian, Muir Commons, Davis, CA

"[McCamant & Durrett Architects'] work is excellent. I find myself quoting them several times a day. The information was valuable and well-presented."
— Joan, Founder Ecovillage, Ithaca, NY

**Books by the Author:**

Cohousing: A Contemporary Approach to Independent Living

Creating Cohousing: Building Sustainable Communities

The Senior Cohousing Handbook: A Community Approach to Independent Living

Growing Community: How to Find New Cohousing Members

Finding A Site: Cohousing From the Ground Up

Happily Ever Aftering In Cohousing: A Handbook for Community Living

Revitalizing Our Small Towns: Recent Examples from Southern France

**Keyword Search:**

Social

Housing

Seniors

Eldering

Aging

Community

Architecture

Habitat Press Publishing
The BookPatch LLC
ISBN 978-0945929048

No part of this document may be reproduced without written permission from McCamant and Durrett Architects.

# Senior Cohousing Primer
## Recent Examples & New Projects

McCamant & Durrett Architects

Charles Durrett and Jean Nilsson

# Table of Contents

**Introduction**    **A Better Way to Age Happily and Well** . . . . . . . . . . . . . . . . . . . . . . . . 1

**Part 1**    **Cohousing As a Model for Aging Successfully** . . . . . . . . . . . . . . . . . . 9

Participation Builds Community

Good Design Maintains Connections over Time

Extensive Common Facilities, Smaller Houses

Self-Management by Cooperation and Consensus

**Part 2**    **Taking Charge of the Future: Workshops and Early Senior Cohousing** . . 21

Study Group 1 Aging Successfully Workshops

Early Senior Cohousing: Four Diverse Examples

**Part 3**    **Living and Aging in Community** . . . . . . . . . . . . . . . . . . . . . . . . . . . . 39

Quality of Life, Sustainability, and Longevity

Staying Healthy in Community: Care and Co-Care

Sharing, Saging, Engagement, and the Value of Elderhood

# Table of Contents

**Part 4**   **Creating Senior Cohousing Communities: Recent Examples** . . . . . . . . . . 49

    Silver Sage Village, Boulder, Colorado

    Wolf Creek Lodge, Grass Valley, California

    Nevada City Cohousing, Nevada City, California:
    Seniors in Intergenerational Cohousing (Calif.)

**Part 5**   **New Projects and Communities in Design** . . . . . . . . . . . . . . . . . . . 65

    Port Townsend, Washington, Quimper Village

    Mountain View, California, Mountain View Cohousing

    Stillwater, Oklahoma, Oakcreek Community

    Shepherdstown, West Virginia, Shepherd Village

    Santa Cruz, California, Walnut Commons

    Fair Oaks, California, Fair Oaks EcoHousing

    Vancouver, British Columbia, Vancouver Cohousing

    Chilliwack, British Columbia, Yarrow Ecovillage

    Durham, North Carolina, Village Hearth Cohousing

    Nevada County, California, Rincon del Rio

    American Canyon, California, Valley View Senior Homes

    Nevada City, California, Opportunity Village

# Introduction
## A Better Way to Age Happily and Well

What does it take to look forward to growing older? How can we make the second fifty years of life as much fun and meaningful as the first fifty?

The second half of life, like the first, can be a time of opportunity and growth. As one of my neighbors puts it, "Cohousing is a great place to be, a great place where family, friends, and neighbors can learn to cook together, learn to listen, and learn to care." Because your friends and neighbors live nearby in cohousing, you have both the time and the proximity to develop deep and meaningful relationships, and laugh. And you will.

Living in cohousing is a profoundly rich experience. All the places for growth and all the things that you didn't do before, or thought you couldn't do, are now easy to do. Imagine going with your neighbor to events like music concerts, movies, and dance festivals. Imagine cooking together, learning about food—how to bake bread, make cheese, brew beer . . . it's a list that goes on forever. Who knew that after you turn fifty, growing tomatoes could become a competitive sport? Once, about fifteen seniors, including myself, were playing music in the common house of our community. After an hour playing covers of Pete Seeger, Johnny Cash, and everything in between, we decided to trade musical instruments. "Everyone hand your guitar, or mandolin, or violin to the person to the right." That's real growth, learning to appreciate what you didn't even suspect you liked. Living in cohousing puts you on the most natural learning curve imaginable.

In cohousing the deep and meaningful conversations grow richer by the month, helping you make sense of this life that we're given, including the crazy politics. No matter how much fun you have, the simple truth is that life is difficult. Again, cohousing provides you with support in meaningful and unexpected ways. In 2015, for example, I experienced a serious medical emergency. Given how debilitated I was at the time, and given the

Photo credit: Oakcreek Community

projected length of my recovery, the doctors said I would need extensive rehab and recommended I go to a skilled nursing facility. But once I explained where I live, that all of the ninety people in my community play an active role in caring for each other, the doctors agreed that the best place for me to go was to my own home. Once there, I received fifteen hours of physical therapy per week, facilitated by my neighbors.

Mitigating the inevitable trials of life is what cohousing does best. When things go sideways, your community will be there to receive you home. Imagine basking in benevolence as you heal—from people you know and trust, people who bring you tea, dinner, and conversation. It is a huge gift when a neighbor comes over to check in on you or read to you.

Community doesn't make the difficulties of life go away, of course. But it does help you manage them. Sharing feelings and commiserating about losses softens the stings of life, just as sharing milestones and celebrating achievements with your family, friends, and neighbors make life sweet.

## Seniors, Housing, Independence, and Community

We have a housing crisis in this country for older adults. Dramatic demographic, economic, and technological changes in our society have created a population that lives longer and ages healthier. But as a society we have not fully come to terms with how and where we will live our later years.

Most people enter their senior years without planning for the realities of getting older. It is as if they presume they

> "In 1950, there were fourteen people aged sixty-five and over in European and American countries for every hundred people of working age. Today there are twenty-eight. The trend is expected to continue for at least the next years years."
>
> — New York Times, December 2015

will not be alone or lonely, always be able to easily get where they need to go, enjoy good health, and otherwise live as they always have. Not planning for aging successfully isn't a strategy, it's wishful thinking.

The simple truth is that successful aging requires good planning. As architects, we consider how appropriate housing, good neighborhoods, and accommodating urban design features can provide a supportive environment for successful and healthy aging. We have learned that seniors need places that facilitate both independence and community, places where neighbors can gather together and share a meal, places that make life easier and richer, and places that keep seniors connected with caring neighbors on a daily basis.

Successful housing solutions for our "youthful-old" seniors must reflect their desire to maintain comfort, control, and independence. Most of us don't have extended families living nearby; we don't have stay-at-home children to take care of us anymore (nor do we want them to); and most of us do not live in a well-connected small town. Today, many older adults continue to live in the single-family homes where they raised their families. Usually, this type of housing is not fit for a successful aging scenario or for a sustainable future. In the typical suburb, the automobile is the de facto extension of the single-family house. Driving is an absolute requirement for a person wanting to conduct business, shop, see friends, or join in social activities.

As we get older, the things we once took for granted aren't so easy to do anymore. The house is older and too big to maintain, a visit to the grocery store or doctor's office is a major expedition, and preparing a healthy meal is a burdensome chore. Nonetheless, many seniors hold on to the notion of aging-in-place. Historically, aging-in-place meant that grandparents lived and died in their own home with extended family members there to value and care for them. Today, it may mean aging and dying alone in the big suburban house, an institution, a hospital, or even on the streets.

The reality is that too many seniors who age-in-place today become isolated, lonely, and inactive. These individuals must rely on costly senior services that lack the companionship and support that an old-fashioned neighborhood or small town can provide. Enter big business. They offer seniors pre-planned, suburban, or resort-style 55+ housing developments, as well as independent- and assisted-living scenarios. Without a doubt, the slick marketing campaigns that sell these housing options are compelling. But the simple truth is that a large pre-planned community does not meet the real long-term needs of today's seniors. It's not community. It's business.

Susan Pinker makes a compelling argument for cohousing in her engaging and persuasive book on how close social bonds and physical proximity are vital to health, resilience and longevity.

Senior cohousing is a proactive solution for successful aging. There are many inspiring and thriving examples of this housing alternative in North America today. Senior cohousing is designed, physically and socially, to make

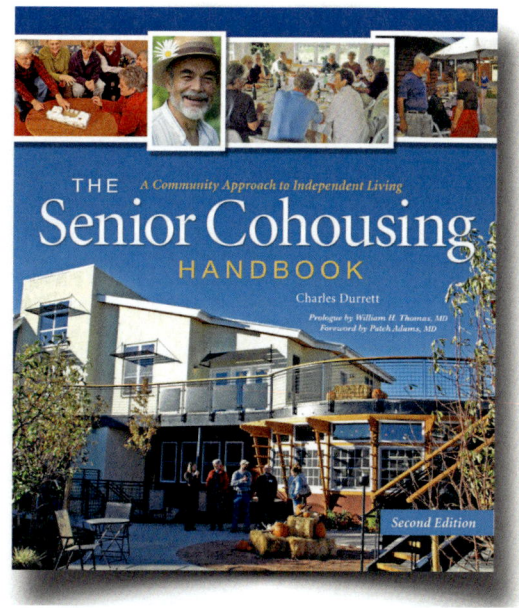

**The Senior Cohousing Handbook, A Community Approach to Independent Living**, 2nd edition, 2009, New Society Publishers, www.newsociety.com, ISBN 978-0-86571-611-7.

> "Principle 1: Live in a community where you know and talk to your neighbors.
>
> All we need to do is picture what our own real, in-person villages might look like, and then reach out to create them."
>
> —Susan Pinker, _The Village Effect: How Face-to-Face Contact Can Make Us Healthier, Happier, and Smarter_.

the second half of life as happy, meaningful, affordable, and enjoyable as the first half. It offers appropriately sized, affordable homes in a community of supportive peers who live right next door to each other. Cohousing and cohousing-inspired communities teach us how to grow old together. They show us that growing older is a natural part of life, and that aging can be a freeing experience rather than an encumbering one.

It's time for the growing number of us who are getting older and living longer to face our realities. It is time for this generation of citizens who have actively and creatively engaged society for the better to redefine the possibilities for even better lives and a better society. It's time now to redefine how we live our later years.

This _Senior Cohousing Primer_ gives you a picture of senior cohousing, its key aspects, and inspiring stories to help you consider the future you want so that you can take action to make it a reality. Once you've gotten a feel for the senior cohousing concept, we encourage you to read _The Senior Cohousing Handbook: A Community Approach to Independent Living_ and our other books and monographs that provide comprehensive information on senior cohousing. If you're still interested in making senior cohousing your reality, take a workshop that uses our _Senior Cohousing Study Group 1: Aging Successfully Workshop Guide_ (see pages 21 and 87 for more information on Study Group 1.)

Then take action.

<u>Senior Cohousing Study Group 1 Aging Successfully Workshop Facilitator Guide</u>, the companion <u>Participant Guide</u>, and our other publications are available on our website: www.cohousingco.com.

# Part 1
# Cohousing As a Model for Aging Successfully

Cohousing incorporates many of the qualities of traditional communities and old-fashioned neighborhoods. Yet cohousing is distinctively contemporary in its approach. Residents make their own decisions, and they choose when and how often to participate in community activities. Relationships are paramount in a cohousing community. Residents live among people with whom they share a common bond of age, experience, and community—a community they themselves designed to specifically meet their own needs. Their community fits them like a glove, unlike a grocery bag (the single family house or 55+ scenarios) or a straightjacket (the assisted-living or nursing home "facilities"). The relationships among residents have proven to afford practical advantages in day-to-day life, supporting purpose and direction and becoming as meaningful as any they've ever had. This is why cohousing for seniors works so well.

## 1. Participation Builds Community

Active participation of residents, from the earliest planning stages through construction and beyond, is the first—and probably the most important—component of cohousing. The desire to live in a vibrant, interactive cohousing community is the driving force to getting it built and making it successful over time. The number of residents who initiate the project and participate throughout the planning and development process varies from project to project. This core group can consist of six, ten, twelve, or more older adults. This group establishes a development program, finds the site, hires the architect, and then seeks other interested people to fill out the community.

Typically, few participants know each other before joining the group. But they quickly get to know each other as they work through the planning and development stages. They must agree on many issues that are closely tied to their personal values. The bonds that form among residents greatly contribute to their community after they move in. Seniors who join later benefit from the culture that is already in place.

Once built, a senior cohousing community provides a small neighborhood where residents can rightly assume that neighbors will participate in the daily life of the place and share expectations about how they will

Participation builds a sense of pride, a common history, camaraderie, and community that no outside developer can build into a project. A feeling of community emerges among the core group of residents during the early period when they are working together to reach their common goal.

Here, I am working with the Oakcreek Community group who explore site design options in a weekend workshop. When groups generate their site plans themselves they have ownership and they'll work harder than any developer to get their project built.

'The basic premise of cohousing—that life is better together than apart—is an even neater fit for people as they age . . . But cohousing communities specifically geared for seniors are just beginning to take off.

"Aging is a team sport," said Dr. Bill Thomas, geriatrician and author of What are Old People For? "For a long time, the team was your blood kin. Now the team, more and more, is going to be the people with whom we choose to live... Elder cohousing is a response to the fading away of our traditional understanding of family and care-giving."

It is also a search for the elusive ideal of community: that remembered or dreamed-of network of people who won't cramp your style but will make sure you're OK as you grow up or grow old.'

—Maria L. La Ganga , LA Times, 2007

cooperate. Interestingly, residents tend to cooperate well beyond any pre-considered limits. They soon discover that cooperation does not diminish their independence nor does it crimp their lifestyle.

In fact, the opposite is true.

## 2. Good Design Maintains Connections over Time

While the participatory development process initiates a sense of community, the physical design facilitates community day to day and sustains it over time. Physical design is critically important in facilitating a long-term social atmosphere. Deliberate design of the physical environment encourages a strong neighborhood atmosphere where residents can interact casually, get to know each other better, and feel secure. A successful design depends largely on the architect's and organizing group's understanding of how design factors affect community life. Without thoughtful consideration, many opportunities are lost. (You can find much more information on achieving a good design in the book Creating Cohousing.)

Pedestrian paths provide places where connections and impromptu plans naturally happen. Nevada City Cohousing residents pass by the common house as they enter or leave the community, and garden areas along the path between houses provides natural places for neighbors to stop for a chat.

**Above**: The common house is the heart of the community, providing a place to gather regularly for morning coffee, common dinners, and many other organized and informal occasions.

The common house and private houses complement each other, offering a choice throughout the day of connecting with others or private time.

## Site Design

Beginning with the initial site plan, residents discuss design aspects that will increase their possibilities for social contact.

Placing parking at the edge of the site allows the majority of the community to be pedestrian-oriented, making it safe for seniors and grandchildren alike. Rather than houses being "across the street" they are placed along common walking paths. This proximity gives a comforting sensibility to the outdoor spaces. A site plan that relegates parking to the periphery downplays the importance of the auto, promotes carpooling, and eliminates the noise and emissions. It encourages walking and the spending of time outdoors. A central path connects clusters of homes to each other and the common facilities.

Cohousing neighborhoods tend to be compact because clustered houses naturally promote community. By clustering, land and resources are used efficiently, preserving open spaces beyond the buildings and allowing the buildings to define positive outdoor spaces that make interactions easy.

As residents enter their community, they pass by the common house and common terrace. The common house features a large kitchen and dining room, which can seat everyone in the community for dinner. This flexible space also provides a place for a variety of activities, both indoors and outdoors. The common house and common terrace act as a traditional town square or village green. Neighbors often meet each other coming and going in these common spaces, and these casual interactions facilitate engagement in activities and conversation.

## A Pedestrian Neighborhood of Paths and Porches

Front porches and front doors overlook the commons paths. The usable porches, which are at least seven feet deep and nine feet wide, are outdoor rooms. They are inexpensive to build and when done right people will frequently use them. Along the walkways to the houses, there are also gathering nodes every five to nine houses.

**Below:** The private house allows each resident to enjoy time alone whenever they choose. A front door and large kitchen window that face the community give the residents a view, from inside their own kitchen, of neighbors coming and going.

Thoughtfully designed private houses address both privacy and connection.

**Below:** The common house and terrace provide a central place for residents to become acquainted, make and share food, discover mutual interests, and share experiences. Common facilities and activities contribute greatly to the formation of a tightly knit community.

A node may feature benches or a picnic table, or it might be a garden area where people can stop for a chat and linger.

### 3. Extensive Common Facilities, Smaller Houses

Each private home is a complete house in and of itself, and the resident owns it just like any traditional home. The common house provides an extension and complement to each private residence. Together, the private

Photo credit: Oakcreek Community

**Right Top:** Residents participate in setting goals and making design decisions in senior cohousing, and the site and common house are completely accessible and comfortable for those of differing ages and abilities.

The common house and private house designs are specifically tailored to seniors, with attention to universal design principals while avoiding an institutional look. In individual homes, every possible interior safety feature does not have to be installed at the outset. Awareness and a simple, flexible house design are more important. Homes can be easily modified to suit owners as they age, and also to accommodate new owners.

**Right Bottom:** Well-designed, energy-efficient, smaller houses are more comfortable, easier for seniors to manage, and less costly to build and maintain.

Open plans feel spacious and well lit, and also work well for addressing reduced mobility as we age.

houses and the common areas give residents the choice, at any time, for as much privacy or as much community as they wish.

## The Common House at the Center of a Neighborhood

The common house and its terrace is the heart of a cohousing community. It is a welcoming and community-sustaining place, much like a Parisian café. It is a place for common dinners, morning coffee, afternoon tea, games on rainy days, a Friday night bar, crafts workshops, celebrations, and numerous organized and informal activities.

Common dinners have proven over time to be an overwhelmingly successful aspect of cohousing. Cohousing groups plan for meals in the common house several times a week, with about half of the residents participating on any given evening. Substantial space is thus allocated in the common house for a pleasant dining room and spacious kitchen.

A common house generally includes a sitting room, guest rooms, laundry room, mail room, and often a workshop, media room, craft room, or music room, depending on the group's desires. Senior cohousing communities put large guest rooms or suites in the common house, which allows for short as well as extended visits from residents' families. These guest suites can also be used to house professional caregivers if residents need help.

In cohousing, the common house is an extension of the individual houses and is an essential part of daily community and even private life. With residents often involved in the larger community, the common house becomes an asset for the surrounding neighborhood as well. It can play host to classes, meetings for local or neighborhood organizations, and cultural programs. These activities connect the cohousing community to the larger neighborhood.

Residents are in charge of running their community and sharing responsibilities. Each community determines its own solutions, making adjustments along the way.

In Munksøgård (above), an early Danish senior community, the residents do most of the work themselves without hiring outside help, work that includes snow clearing, house maintenance, landscaping, tree planting, and work in the vegetable gardens.

Over time, this group has even painted the exteriors of the houses themselves, built a workshop, a storage shed, a greenhouse, a clothes-drying shed and a hen house. While the younger seniors painted the houses (with considerable assistance from neighbors and their own children), the older residents cooked and made coffee for the group.

Seniors contribute to common gardens and plantings along paths without having to be solely responsible for the upkeep. (Nevada City Cohousing, below.) Contributing to these ongoing tasks helps keep people active and engaged, and is of great importance to the social life in the community.

Older seniors often work fewer hours than the younger ones, or they do less physically demanding work. It is often surprising, when motivated, how much they do.

## Private Houses Within a Neighborhood

Because guest rooms, workshops, laundry rooms, and other common facilities are located in the common house—and because many meals, socializing, and entertainment takes place there—the private houses in cohousing can be smaller than typical houses. For many seniors, cohousing is a best-of-both-worlds experience—the smaller houses allow them to downsize their private space while the common facilities provide them all the amenities of a larger home.

Some seniors initially feel reluctant about moving into a cohousing community. They wonder if they will have too little privacy. This is an unfounded concern because loneliness and isolation are the more common experiences associated with aging. Thoughtfully designed private houses can strike the perfect balance between privacy and connection. Kitchens are placed near the front porch and entry, while more private areas—living rooms and bedrooms—typically face the rear, private side of the house. These private spaces often open to a small backyard or porch that offers a quiet outdoor space for the resident.

## 4. Self-Management by Cooperation and Consensus

Cooperation and consensus aren't required when living alone or in an institution, but they're crucial for the creation and growth of a senior community, for getting along with others over time, and for garnering the support and love to age happily. In contrast to losing one's autonomy in assisted care, seniors in cohousing remain in charge.

In keeping with the spirit in which cohousing is built, residents—owners and renters alike—are responsible for the community's ongoing management. The common house and common spaces are owned in common by all residents, typically similar to a condominium project. Otherwise, there is no shared common economy. Cohousing is about how people can live together, rather than any particular financing or ownership scheme.

## Working Together in the Community

Cohousing groups are unusual in that they are not hierarchical. This organizational structure is designed to give each of the members of the community a voice in decisions that affect the community. Group members participate in designing their own community; they decide how the group will function and what features are most important to them. This is one of the most appealing aspects of cohousing, but it is also challenging because it is a way of functioning that is unfamiliar to many people who are used to authoritarian, competitive, and bureaucratic styles of organization. Our hierarchical culture does not prepare us to work together in a community. We have to learn the powerful, and often new, skills of group process, compassionate communication, and group facilitation. These skills are fundamental to successful consensus-based decision-making, where no one person dominates the decisions or the community-building process, and where no one person is excessively taxed by the process. Over time, you and your neighbors can learn to listen and work with each other to garner the best solutions. All you need is the willingness to grow and learn by doing.

Responsibilities are typically divided among work groups, and all adults participate in making the community run smoothly, as decided by the group. Cooking common dinners and cleaning the common house are usually rotated. This division of labor is based on what each person feels he or she can fairly contribute, and in senior cohousing, age and ability are taken into consideration. As a group, residents can hire professionals to perform tasks that require technical expertise, such as electrical work or building maintenance.

Major decisions are made at common meetings, usually held once a month. These meetings provide a forum for residents to discuss issues and solve problems. The group may adopt organizational formats developed by other groups or create new methods for themselves. Over time communities become effective at working together.

# Part 2
## Taking Charge of the Future: Workshops and Early Senior Cohousing

When Danish seniors were frustrated by available housing options in the 1980s, they took charge and began creating a housing type that redefined the concept of neighborhood to fit contemporary lifestyles. From their efforts, the first senior cohousing communities were created. Twenty years later, groups in the U.S. began similar journeys. Looking at a few of these early examples will give you a sense of the people, their dreams, and the processes that helped them create places that offer life-enhancing experiences every day.

### Aging Successfully Workshops

Danes initiated Study Group 1 Aging Successfully (SG1) Workshops to explore the challenges and opportunities of aging successfully and aging-in-place. Facilitated by teachers—not gerontologists or academics, but people who knew how to listen and promote discussion—these workshops were a forum where seniors discussed the issues they faced, shared concerns and joys, and worked together to discover the best ways to enjoy life. Many participants felt that older adults were being institutionalized too early, either because they were lonely—often isolated in their homes—and/or because they needed minor assistance, such as with grocery shopping. The evening classes were geared to help older people solve these problems and age successfully at home. They did not initially focus on cohousing as a solution.

Preliminary discussions focused primarily on raising consciousness and understanding what would happen to their emotions, their bodies, their minds, their finances,

The first Danish senior cohousing group who founded Midgården in 1985 in Copenhagen, above.

Danes in SG1 Workshops began exploring the challenges and opportunities of aging in place and the inherent advantages of living in a close-knit community. Their efforts led to the first senior cohousing communities.

The above group met at Silver Sage Village in Boulder, Colorado, in 2009.

In recent years, at SG1 Facilitator Training Workshops held in the U.S., many seniors interested in starting a senior cohousing group in their own community, or in facilitating SG1 Workshops for other groups, have explored similar issues of aging-in-place and received training to facilitate these workshops.

and their friends as they aged. As the course progressed, the facilitators saw how people struggled to deal with the reality of their current—and future—situations, and how that internal conflict kept them from aging happily and safely. While most seniors had prepared wills and put their financial issues in order, they had neglected to consider where they would get social support if their spouses died or if they lost the ability to drive.

The facilitators listened as participants discussed these issues and explored their choices. Not only were seniors supporting each other as they brainstormed possibilities and solutions, the exploratory process became one of self-discovery.

> Rather quickly, the Danes realized that the highest quality of life could be found in a community of peers who care about each other's well-being. Early SG1 Workshop participants in the U.S. concluded the same.

Participants were asking themselves who they wanted around them in their senior years, what housing and support might look like, and how they could bring about the changes they envisioned.

The participants gradually realized that they had to take charge of their lives and stay socially connected. They realized that, without proactive steps, most seniors become progressively more isolated.

With an understanding of the possibilities and limitations facing them, the participants considered their current housing options. These were largely limited to remaining at home, moving to a smaller home or apartment, or moving in with family or friends.

About 40 percent of those who completed early SG1 Workshops joined newly forming cohousing groups or moved into existing senior cohousing communities. Others moved back to the small towns they grew up in, moved closer to their adult children, moved in with a sibling, or retrofitted their home with grab bars. Regardless, all of them took some action.

## Nielsen's Three-Phase Study Group Model

Since 1985, many senior cohousing communities have been built with a three-phase study group model that evolved from these early workshops, developed by Henry Nielsen. Among Nielsen's goals were to make senior cohousing an option for everyone and to develop a participatory process that would foster strong communities. Nielsen's model has proved to be a very effective method for groups, and we describe it in detail in The Senior Cohousing Handbook. For the purposes of this book, which is a primer on senior cohousing, a closer look at the SG1 Workshop is in order.

## Study Group 1 Aging Successfully Workshop

The first vital task when thinking about aging-in-place is discovering the right place to age successfully. A SG1 Workshop allows seniors to explore issues of aging, housing, and community. This workshop is designed to help participants consider the housing options available to them, including senior cohousing. Through a SG1

Group members in Stillwater, Oklahoma, enjoyed reading together Ciji Ware's book Rightsizing Your Life as they planned their transition to cohousing.

They embraced the idea that smaller private homes would simplify their lives and work well in a supportive community that included common facilities.

They found that selling, handing-down, recycling, and donating extra furniture and possessions from the too-big house before moving to senior cohousing was a liberating experience in itself.

"When I retired, I looked around Stillwater to see what housing options were available for me as I thought about moving out of my big house. There really were no options that appealed to me. As I explored the cohousing concept, I was intrigued with the potential of living in a community where people share values and encourage each other to fully live into these values. Joining with a group of people who were also interested in creating a cohousing community was the beginning of a new learning experience and a journey of faith and trust. The result is Oakcreek Community, and I love living here.

Sharing the fun times and having the security of knowing that my neighbors really do care about me and will come to my aid when I need a hand is great. As I share my talents in community work teams I feel valued knowing that collectively we are creating a place where quality of life remains high."

—*Kay Stewart, resident, Oakcreek Community*

Workshop, you can discover if moving into a senior cohousing community is the right choice for you.

Typically held in weekly 90-minute sessions with 10 or 12 people, a SG1 Workshop provides a supportive context and a strong foundation for becoming familiar and comfortable with a group process. (For detailed information on the process, see our Senior Cohousing Study Group 1 Aging Successfully: Workshop Facilitator Guide and our Participant Guide.)

Participating in SG1 makes vivid the opportunities, challenges, and difficulties of aging-in-place. It also reveals the advantages that aging in community offers in comparison to the alternatives.

One of the most gratifying processes of the entire SG1 Workshop is looking inside of yourself and discovering what's there. As many participants learn, successful aging comes from a conscious commitment to continue their self-education as well as to develop a new set of life-enhancing

strategies. They learn that successful aging is a choice, that it means making a conscious commitment to continue their self-education and to develop a new set of skills and strategies, including resilience and directness. Establishing integrity—integrating one's life experiences and achieving self-acceptance—is critical in attaining fulfillment and inner contentment.

Experts in gerontology make a clear distinction between passive aging and successful aging. The isolation of seniors not only propagates a poor quality of life for them, it affects our entire society on every level. As taxpayers we pay for unsustainable and inefficient services; as adult children of aging seniors we bear emotional and financial stress; as future seniors and grandparents we face a potentially grim future. Seniors do not want to be a burden on either society or their children, and they do not want to be pushed aside. Rather they wish to be participating members of their families, and want to continue to grow and contribute to society. Indeed, the interlaced web of our society—which at its best relies on reciprocal interrelationships of elders, adults, and children—suffers when our elders suffer.

Participants in SG1 Workshops step back and take a good look inward and then look ahead into the future. They discuss—with their peers—the realities of aging and mortality, the issues of aging in place, the issues of isolation, the issues and benefits of living in community. They learn about their choices, and they create a personal vision of what aging successfully will entail.

### Early Senior Cohousing: Four Diverse Examples

In 1982, two Danish women, Tove Duvå and Lissy Lund Hansen, started to campaign for independent-oriented housing for seniors. They referenced a successful model that was already in place: Cohousing. The women succeeded in finding a nonprofit housing developer, Lejerbo, who was willing to attempt the

project. In 1987, they completed Midgården, the first senior cohousing community. The public response to this new development was overwhelmingly positive. Hundreds attended forums sponsored by a nonprofit organization called Quality of Living in Focus, and the result was the formation of a new agency, the Organization of Senior Cohousing, whose mission was to educate the public about this housing option.

Munksøgård Senior Cohousing (left) is one of five communities built on the site of an existing farm in Denmark (as shown in overall site plan, lower right).

The senior group decided, for economic reasons, to build two-story buildings, comfortable with the knowledge that, with cooperation, the stairs would not be a problem. This variety of units has worked well for the residents.

The senior cohousing movement spread rapidly throughout Denmark, led by proactive, enterprising seniors themselves and not by the government, investors, or other professionals. Since its inception, they have established more than 350 senior cohousing communities in Denmark, a country of 5 million. The movement quickly spread to Sweden and the Netherlands, and the U.S. was not far behind.

## Munksøgård: Senior Cohousing amid a Larger Community

Munksøgård senior cohousing in Roskilde, Denmark, completed in 2000, is a very successful community of twenty units. The community was initiated in 1995 as part of a large new cohousing project by a group of environmentalists from Copenhagen who envisioned a community with significant diversity in the ages and backgrounds of the residents: older and younger, high and low-income, quiet and gregarious, and big families as well as singles. One of the five communities proposed for this large project would feature a 20-unit community for seniors over fifty years of age. A broad variety of common facilities and activities would draw people together in their daily lives and establish the sense of community that characterizes a village. In short, it would become a modern version of the traditional village, one that pointed toward the future and could inspire others. The group also wanted this project to sustain both environmental and social ecologies, and included specific goals to achieve a 20 percent decrease in water consumption and to make the cohousing community essentially nonpolluting.

Once the group had agreed on their program, they connected with Copenhagen architects Nielsen & Rubow, a firm well experienced with cohousing. The group found a large rural site outside the university town of Roskilde, near a station on the commuter train line to Copenhagen. Nielsen & Rubow developed an initial feasibility plan with houses laid out in a circle around an existing farm. The site featured a central courtyard with car parking relegated to the periphery. The farm, Munksøgård (the monk's garden), was to serve as a common building for all the residents, and the group agreed on the importance of quality common meals. A large part of the site was to remain undeveloped, partly as a recreational area and partly as a vegetable garden.

The Munksøgård senior group wanted to live in proximity to communities with children, and this concept has worked well for them. Parties for two or three, or even all five of the communities are popular. Yet the seniors remain relatively self-contained and don't rely much on the neighboring communities. They prefer to enjoy their most important common activity—their common dinners in the common house, five nights a week—separately from the other groups.

### Korvetten: Cohousing for Retiring Steelworkers

Korvetten Cohousing, completed in 1998, is a senior cohousing community of sixteen rental units in Munkebo, Denmark (population, 5,740). In 1996, the municipality proposed a cohousing

project to address the needs of retiring steel workers who had moved to the town from all over Denmark in the 1960s to work at the then-expanding local shipyard. The municipality contacted the nonprofit Quality of Living in Focus, and together with Henry Nielsen, they arranged a public information meeting to gauge interest in creating senior cohousing. Local interest exceeded expectations, and forty-two individuals joined SG1 Aging Successfully Workshops facilitated by Nielsen (provided in two separate sessions).

The advantages for the municipality were obvious, and the city council voted unanimously to support projects on two sites. The seniors would have a better quality of life and need less in-home care if they lived together in a supportive community.

The first resident group had twenty-two members ages fifty-two to seventy-eight. Their SG1 Workshop was successful beyond expectations, with group members bonding strongly early in the process, sharing confidences and soon initiating parties, trips, and even an annual Summer Solstice Party. This group became a community long before move-in.

The city allowed the resident group to choose the architect and developer themselves, and to participate in making the mandatory local area development plan for the site, which is beautifully situated on the Kertinge Bay. As it so happens, the site is also close to a supermarket, a doctor's office, and public transportation.

The seniors and the architect designed the project as five one-story buildings, with private houses and a common house surrounding a large common yard. Placed near the perimeter parking lot, the common house serves as an entrance to the community. The small private houses (625–900 square feet) all have front doors facing the central yard, and from the large windows in the private kitchens, residents can follow what is happening outside.

Complementing the small houses is the common house with its large dining-living room, kitchen, laundry, guest room, siting area, and storage space. In June 1998, the residents moved in to their new senior cohousing community, which they named Korvetten after an old type of ship.

Korvetten remains a well-functioning senior cohousing community today, and the tight-knit resident group runs their own community. All involved agree that Korvetten would not have been built so successfully without the three-phase study group method and the deliberate community-building processes it produces.

## First Senior Cohousing in America: Glacier Circle

The pioneering Glacier Circle Community is an inspirational and instructive example for senior cohousing groups.

Between 2002 and 2006, a group of friends in Davis, California, successfully completed the first small senior cohousing community of eight units—with the average resident age of eighty—relying on their collective initiative, hard work, and vision. Their community was based on strong friendships and faith in finding a better housing solution to support successfully aging in place.

Members of this group were retirees—a schoolteacher, painter, physicist, college professor, environmental health scientist, psychotherapist, and psychologist. They were in their mid-seventies to early nineties, and many had known each other for forty to fifty years. Many were also members of the Unitarian Universalist (UU) Church, some of them founding members, and the women were

As one Glacier Circle resident simply put it, "Living here has meant I can be the best friend I always wanted to be to my best friend."

**We, the members of Glacier Circle, covenant:**

To listen deeply and thoughtfully in our dialogues, mindful that our relationships are sacred.

To be patient with each other, appreciating our differing gifts and welcoming creative ideas. When necessary, we will confront courageously with love.

We agree to assume appropriate leadership roles and to participate fully in the group process.

While we value our time together, we also respect our members' need for privacy.

We will remember to assume the good intent of others and to strive to treat other members as well as ourselves with loving-kindness.

---

members of a long-standing women's group that became a safe place to share concerns about aging, isolation, driving, providing care for a spouse, institutionalization, and "who would take care of us when it got to that point."

They shared their frustrations in taking care of a large, empty house—appropriate for raising their family but not for growing old in—and easily imagined that they would feel increasingly isolated in that house in their later years. They considered different options, including the university retirement community, co-ops, buying bungalows together, or renovating a huge house. When Ellen Coppock invited the women and husbands of her women's group and others from the UU Church for a gathering at her home, "two dozen people filled up my living room." Among them was Muir Commons Cohousing developer Virginia Thigpen, who became an advisor to the project.

Over time, the group concluded that senior cohousing would give them both the independence and the proximate community they needed to age in place successfully. They participated in facilitation training at the local university, learning about each other's strengths and challenges in the process. After hiring a developer consultant and an architect, they embarked on developing their senior community. They chose a site with public transit and shops nearby. It was also within walking distance of a greenbelt area that featured a walking path and wildlife pond. A major hospital was a few blocks away. Four years after they began their planning, the residents were able to move in and enjoy their rich relationships close at hand.

A common garden with vegetables, citrus and fruit trees unites the three buildings with their eight houses and common house. They have common dinners four times a week in the common house, utilizing its large kitchen and dining area with common terrace facing a common courtyard. Above the common house, they included an affordable second floor apartment (900 square feet) to be used in the future for an on-site nurse to help residents age in place. They thought it would be two

years before they would look for an on-site caregiver, but actually they hired a caregiver within two months after moving in.

When we asked founding members Ellen and Ray what they would have done differently, they concurred, "We really wish we would have started this earlier. It would have been great to start aging in community by the age of sixty or sixty-five. If we could share one piece of advice to those considering senior cohousing, it would be: Just do it!"

**ElderSpirit: Spiritual, Mutually Supportive, Affordable**

Spirituality can be an incredible source of strength for seniors and a great common focus for a community. Many seniors use spirituality to reach greater insight and self-awareness, either through established religions, spiritual practices, or through activities like yoga or tai-chi.

ElderSpirit in Abingdon, Virginia, is a 29-unit mixed-income community that was completed in 2006. ElderSpirit grew out of a nonprofit organization started in 1967 by a group of women working in Appalachia with the Federation of Communities in Service (FOCIS), a community service and development effort.

In 1995, a group of potential residents were nearing retirement age. They began to explore the idea of creating a senior cohousing community specifically for people ages 55+ who regarded their senior years as a phase brimming with possibilities, and who were interested in late-life spirituality and mutual support as a framework for a community.

The group decided to place their community in Abingdon. With the help of Dene Peterson, they found a 3.7-acre site along the Virginia Creeper Trail. They formed the Trailview Development Corporation to purchase the property, and FOCIS received a 3-year grant from The Retirement Research Foundation of Chicago for predevelopment expenses, enabling them to establish a board,

## ElderSpirit Mission Statement

Spirituality: Members believe that spiritual growth is the primary work of those in the later stages of life. Members encourage one another in the search for meaning in life and commitment to a spiritual path. Freedom of religion is fundamental.

Mutual Support: Members develop face-to-face relationships through which they offer and receive support. They express their needs and convictions, listen to each other and strive to act responsibly, considering their good and the good of the other.

Simple Lifestyle and Respect for the Earth: Conscious that over-consumption by persons in wealthy countries threatens the earth's living systems, members seek a simplified lifestyle that reflects a respectful relationship with the environment.

Arts and Recreation: Leisure, recreational activities, and travel contribute uniquely toward refreshing the mind, body and spirit. The arts form an integral part of the community. Members share and develop their gifts and talents through such activities as music, dance, theater, storytelling, gardening, crafts, weaving, etc.

Health: The word "health" comes from the same root as "heal," "whole," and "holy." Recognizing this, members pay attention to nutrition, rest, exercise and social interaction.

hire staff, and engage an architect. Project manager Dene Peterson contacted government housing agencies to find ways to make affordable housing a part of the project, and community coordinator Jean Marie Luce got the word out and gathered prospective residents, primarily through classes for older adults taught at the local college.

Construction began in 2004, and in the summer of 2006 residents moved into their new community, which features twenty-nine homes—thirteen privately owned one- and two-bedroom attached units and sixteen income-restricted rental homes—along pedestrian paths with a centrally located common house, a spiritual center, and a plaza. Parking is placed at the edges of the site.

ElderSpirit has created a lot of interest, inspiring people to create similar spiritual communities all over the U.S. and Canada. ElderSpirit Community in Abingdon now includes an organization for seniors that works on the formation of senior communities and spiritual programs.

Copyright © 2018 McCamant & Durrett Architects

# Part 3
# Living and Aging in Community

## Quality of Life, Sustainability, and Longevity

There is tremendous value in having people in our lives with whom we have long-term relationships, who we know and trust, and who live near us. As social beings, we benefit from having others in our immediate environment who listen and share daily happenings.

As we age, those with whom we share a variety of pleasures—music, gardening, hiking, traveling, or discussing a good book—keep us healthy. A clear, stimulated mind, personal warmth, and reciprocal support play a big role in preventing physical, mental, and emotional ailments.

Living in community fosters emotional social strength. Cohousing encourages residents to express their views and preferences. In turn, these individuals become more outspoken and less self-conscious over time. Community living motivates us to stretch our independence, learn new skills, and rediscover the creativity and playfulness of our youth.

Senior cohousing re-creates a village-like environment where residents stay happier and healthier longer.

## Top Ten Reasons Seniors Live in Cohousing

### 1. Health

Social connections promote engaging in physical activities, and these connections provide a sense of purpose and well-being. Social connections extend life because they give people a reason to stay fit, active, and engaged, and make it easy to do so on a daily basis.

## 2. Safety and Security

Residents of cohousing form meaningful relationships with their neighbors. From those relationships they achieve safety and security. A common refrain goes like this: "Before living in a senior cohousing community, very few of our neighbors were home during the day. And sometimes we felt vulnerable. In cohousing we know there are people here who will check in on us if we don't show up at the usual time. It takes away that worry that no one will miss you."

## 3. Community

A strong, supportive community is an important factor in successful aging. Everyone wants to feel welcome in a place that supports camaraderie and mutual respect. Community makes life more interesting and fun. A sense of belonging, identity, and accountability are all basic ingredients of the good life.

"The next Buddha will not take the form of an individual. The next Buddha may take the form of a community—a community practicing understanding and loving kindness, a community practicing mindful living. This may be the most important thing we can do for the survival of the Earth."

— *Thich Nhat Hanh*

## 4. Avoid Becoming a Burden

Almost every senior with children has been heard to say, "I don't want to be a burden to my children." Today, adult children live farther away from their parents than ever before, but they still feel the need to come home. In senior cohousing, because neighborhood life unfolds just outside the front door, those adult children are relieved from feeling like they have to do things for their parents when they visit. Instead of spending their visit making repairs, cleaning the house, and taking care of neglected business, because of cohousing they are free to spend time engaged with their parents. For most children—and their elderly parents—these visits become a chance to combine joy with a sense of freedom.

## 5. Food

In senior cohousing, you can live alone yet not need to cook or eat every meal alone. Not only do common dinners provide variety and companionship, the immediate proximity to friends makes it easy to share meals with a few neighbors. Good food, shared with friends, is the spice of life.

## 6. Impact on the Planet

Senior cohousing affords a chance to tread much more lightly on the planet. Shared resources means many of the environmental aspirations that residents have can finally be achieved. Many residents in senior cohousing find great satisfaction in a community where they are part of the solution.

## 7. Kindred Spirits

Senior cohousing allows people to build a community of peers. Even in intergenerational neighborhoods, seniors may find themselves among young people who are not that familiar with events—like the Vietnam War—that had a large influence on their lives.

## 8. Home Maintenance

When upkeep on an old house isn't fun anymore, when it costs too much, when the quality of hired-out work is suspect, then it's time to think about moving on.

## 9. An Appropriate House

People who want to downsize to a smaller house want it to fit their needs like a glove. Houses in senior cohousing communities are cozier, more accessible, more energy efficient, and cheaper to live in than traditional housing. In addition, the community's common house allows residents to live big while living small.

## 10. Financial Good Sense

Living in senior cohousing costs less—a lot less—than the alternatives. Sharing resources and not having to maintain a big house are obvious money savers. Senior cohousing can be about one-half as expensive as traditional alternatives.

## Staying Healthy in Community: Care and Co-Care

In embracing a healthy aging scenario, people moving into senior cohousing should discuss and address the common concern of what will happen to them as they get older and need assistance taking care of themselves. These care and co-care agreements are an important component for creating a healthy, resident-managed senior cohousing community.

> "Our reluctance to honestly examine the experience of aging and dying has increased the harm we inflict on people and denied them the basic comforts they most need. Lacking a coherent view of how people might live successfully all the way to their very end we have allowed our fate to be controlled by the imperatives of medicine, technology, and strangers."
>
> —Atul Gawande, <u>Being Mortal</u>

Most co-care involves simple shopping errands and minor favors. Simply knowing that neighbors are there for each other, if needed, is the glue that bonds community expectations. However, experts and laypersons alike argue for written agreements about the expectations of co-care and mutual favors within a given senior cohousing community. Elaborate contracts aren't always needed. The Munksøgård seniors, for example, have chosen to have very few written co-care agreements; instead, the residents decide these limits for themselves along the way—for instance, three people with cars agree to drive others to the hospital in case of an emergency.

### 1. Co-Care: What We Agree to Do for Each Other

The care you agree to do for your neighbor may include things like bringing them dinner, driving them to appointments, making tea, helping them shop, or keeping them company.

This kind of caregiving is easier to do for people who live near you. You are also more likely to feel like giving and receiving these kinds of care when they are performed by neighbors who know each other and who are concerned for each other's well-being. "We look after each other. We eat together, talk together, and are interested in each other," Olaf Dejgaard, a Munksøgård resident noted.

As his neighbor Hedda Lundh put it, "You get hooked into having all these people living around you. If you're ill, they bring up food, and you're constantly asked if there's anything they can do for you."

## 2. Co-Care: The Unexpected

In a community, relationships grow into meaningful friendships. Like small town neighbors, cohousing residents find themselves not thinking twice about helping out when a neighbor asks for a favor. The sense of community allows this to happen. Community and proximity naturally promote co-care and enable the emotional support that plays such a key role in prevention and recovery.

Appended to their mission statement, ElderSpirit resident members stated the following values and goal:

### Care during Illness and Dying:

The common goal of the ElderSpirit cohousing community is to offer care to one another in the later years. It affirms home care and dying at home.

However, when institutional care occurs, a member of the community stays in touch with the person and closely follows her/his condition. Members recognize that the process of living involves one's desire for tolerable health and a capacity to be generative.

Within the community, the process of dying raises one's awareness that all surrender physical life, not in isolation, but as a sister or brother of the human community.

Dejgaard explained, "It's so easy to do someone's laundry, if needed. We do some shopping, lots of small errands. But all the intimate stuff—dressing, bathing—we leave to professionals. This means that what we do can remain loosely defined."

### 3. Outside Care

Bringing outside care providers into a cohousing community, for residents who need it, has a number of benefits. First, most of the care can be shared, making it a more affordable option. Second, the care is managed by the community residents, who hire and fire caregivers. Third, with the added support of outside care, the quality of care is higher.

Most seniors do not want to assist each other with personal needs like bathing, dressing, and toileting. Even spouses or other immediate family members who want to assist may not be physically able to do so. These kinds of assistance are usually designated for hired caregivers. With adequate in-home care, seniors can often delay or completely avoid the need for moving to an assisted-living facility or nursing home. Most senior cohousing communities include a small unit that can serve as a so-called caregiver unit. This unit allows a caregiver to live on-site when or if that becomes necessary.

Senior cohousing residents can and do rely on each other, but they all agree that no one is obligated to take care of another member in a particular instance, and everyone agrees not to take advantage of the good will of others.

Mostly, cohousing residents accept their neighbors as they are. The first time I visited Kai, a resident of another cohousing community, in 2001, he was fine. The last time, in 2011, he had dementia. He had dinner with the group, and I sat next to him. The conversation waxed and waned, in and out of focus. I then realized that we all have dementia, it's just a matter of degree. All told, Kai probably lived at home amongst his community at least ten years longer than he would have if he'd lived in a single-family house.

As in old-fashioned neighborhoods and small towns, a history of living in proximity and knowing each other well

goes a long way in taking care of small favors and providing temporary assistance until a longer-term solution is put in place, if necessary. The small things that naturally occur in community make a big difference in recovery and sustaining quality of life.

## Sharing, Saging, Engagement, and the Value of Elderhood

The world needs to hear the wisdom of its elders. As we grow older, we review our lives and harvest those experiences that have the most worth. For some, spirituality may take on a broader meaning and value. For many, it seems that they mostly need to elder each other.

Aging gives us the opportunity to look back on our lives with greater perspective and understanding. Cohousing provides a significant and supportive community environment where seniors can find empowerment and opportunities to express themselves and share their wisdom.

---

The elder years are important—not only for the elderly but for the wider community.

Dr. Bill Thomas, well-known geriatrician and social activist, suggests that the late life tasks of elders are:

- Peace-Making
- Wisdom-Giving
- Legacy-Creation

---

Many seniors take the time to reflect on events that have enhanced and brought joy, meaning, and wisdom to their lives. They often consider how other issues that are more difficult to integrate—an unresolved relationship, a lost opportunity, a personal loss—in retrospect may have provided them with positive opportunities. This reflection allows seniors to make peace with those things that were not a blessing, and in so doing they can let go of those things and move forward.

1. Seniors who live in proximity to caring peers have the opportunity to continue to learn from each other and develop new interests.

2. Seniors living in cohousing educate their peers so that their values and responsibilities form part of their legacy. Seniors need to elder each other as much as they need to elder the youth. It seems that people learn more from their peers than anyone else. They encourage each other to embrace elderhood and to offer their families and the wider world the wisdom that they have acquired through their life experiences.

3. Seniors living in cohousing make a considerable contribution to living more lightly on the planet. They take seriously the adage: "Find a place to inhabit and to steward."

> Cohousers use less water and energy. They create less trash. They encourage each other to recycle and to be conscious about saving resources. They are a model for the larger community.

4. Seniors who live in community are able to affirm daily the importance of the elder years and empower each other to live meaningful and full lives. They reject the cultural and media-imposed images that put forth the idea that old age is only about infirmity, decline, and inevitable isolation.

5. Seniors in a cohousing community live close to their peers and remain socially engaged with their neighbors simply by walking out their doors, sitting on their porches, or sharing meals and activities in the common house. The senior cohousing setting makes it much easier for seniors to be active and engaged in local politics and activities. This process often begins with one resident inviting another to come along on an activity, or simply to take a walk where they can share their involvements and interests. These informal, natural interactions create new opportunities for elders to become more viable members of society.

# Part 4
# Creating Senior Cohousing Communities: Recent Examples

Senior cohousing has been built by community groups in a wide variety of building types, styles, and sites—urban, suburban, and rural—in locations across America and Northern Europe.

Many cohousing communities contain several or more buildings comprising attached dwellings of three or four units. These buildings are clustered around a common house and connected by pedestrian-oriented outdoor spaces and walkways. A few cohousing communities consist of detached single-family houses or duplexes, though these are exceptions because the houses are too spread out, are less energy efficient, and are not conducive to creating a walkable neighborhood. Other cohousing communities are contained in a single large building. Communities in cold northern climates have been built with a central glass-covered pedestrian street to allow access between residences and the common house without needing to go outside.

**Above:** Windsong's central glass-covered pedestrian street provides a well-used outdoor space that greatly extends the opportunities in a cold, wet climate for life between the buildings. This is a benefit for all residents, and especially for seniors.

**Right:** Site plan of long single building at Windsong Cohousing, with central common house.

Cohousing is often new construction, although several communities have adapted old factory buildings or started with a group of existing houses. In one case, residents renovated nine dilapidated row houses to create a charming community in an inner city.

In both Denmark and Sweden, even high-rises and sections of huge housing projects have been partially converted to cohousing. In all scenarios, the private units can be clustered around a common house as the focal point.

## Silver Sage Village
## Boulder, Colorado

Silver Sage Village, completed in 2007, is a successful and thriving mixed-income, sustainable, small-scale community—sixteen units on less than an acre—where people know one another and where mutual support is close at hand. The architectural design, based on participatory workshops with the resident group, facilitates community and provides a sustainable and affordable

"For seniors, cohousing is really retirement housing for those who don't want to ever retire from living a proactive, meaningful and mindful life.

Many of the issues important to seniors are inherent in the lifestyle of the cohousing neighborhood including: convenience and security, healthy social interaction, sharing life experiences, efficient use of time and money resources, and knowing that neighbors are ready and willing to help in most any situation. Being closer to neighbors generates an enriched life that is especially important to us in later life.

This social enrichment promotes a healthier lifestyle as we age together. Being able to walk out your door and see friendly neighbors, and in a few steps to be in the common grounds and the common house all add convenience and a certain social satisfaction and benefit to everyone."

—Jim Leach, Silver Sage resident, 2014

setting that truly supports meaningful, healthful, and satisfying elder years.

Like a traditional small town, Silver Sage is designed to provide support for its senior residents by cooperative, caring neighbors. Its purpose, as the resident group agreed in their mission statement, is the "nurturing and encouraging of people's desire to keep learning, growing, and participating."

**Right:** The common house at Silver Sage, located at the center of the lower level, spills out to a large terrace, connecting paths and gardens. All of these features work to encourage informal daily interaction.

Residents frequently share common dinners in the common house, and also enjoy opportunities for lectures, films, concerts, reading groups, meetings, and fitness together.

The Silver Sage community is a small custom neighborhood within the larger Holiday Neighborhood in North Boulder, which also includes Wild Sage Cohousing. Its street front engages the senior cohousing community with the surrounding neighborhood, while the courtyard side frames a common landscape for the residents. Small porches provide "soft edges" and places of interaction between private and public spaces. The architecture's modern form and roof line fit its inspiring mountain setting.

Individual residences are all ownership units, grouped in one building, around a central common house. Six units are permanently affordable per the City of Boulder's affordable housing program. The private houses are supplemented by a central 3,900-square-foot common house that features a large common kitchen, dining area, living room, crafts and performance areas, mail and posting area, and guest rooms. It also includes provision for a caregiver unit if and when residents decide it is needed for that purpose.

> **Right and Far Right:** Since all the units overlook the common landscape, it's easy for residents to see what's going on and join in a bike ride, a gardening activity, or a chat.

## Wolf Creek Lodge
## Grass Valley, California

Wolf Creek Lodge is a thriving thirty-unit senior community. It was completed in 2012 in Grass Valley, California (pop. 11,500), by a group of older adults who envisioned, developed, and now live in a supportive Sierra Foothills cohousing community. The participatory process engendered a committed group that weathered an economic recession and unusual delays.

This group brought new life to a challenging site in an area that was largely automobile-focused, but within walking distance of the historic downtown and a creekside trail. The central common house and all units overlook the sunny common terrace and reserved open space that leads to the creek.

**Right:** The common house and all private units overlook a common terrace and garden on the building's private courtyard side.

### Wolf Creek Lodge Vision Statement

We at Wolf Creek Lodge are a group of independent, active adults who have come together to create a supportive community in which we can age safely and live fully with dignity and humor.

Inspired by the splendid serene and natural setting in which we live, we strive to be responsible stewards dedicated to sustaining our physical environment.

While acknowledging that each of us holds dear our personal views and beliefs, it is our individual commitment to the core values and goals we share that unite and guide us. In a community fostered by patience, open-mindedness, respect and trust, we enjoy a cooperative, harmonious way of living, full of laughter and joyful community. Together, we learn and grow, sharing a strong sense of belonging and a heartfelt experience of coming home.

**Clockwise from near right:** Future residents discuss design options for their common house at the Common House Workshop; The private house is warm and looks out to nature; Senior cohousing community on the street corner of an 8-acre site, planned to include an intergenerational community, single family homes, and three acres of dedicated open space by the creek; Completed common house kitchen.

**Facing page:** Front porches provide the perfect place for senior residents to enjoy impromptu visits with neighbors, young and old. (upper photos)

Seniors enjoy common dinner with each other on the common house terrace (bottom left) and a walk together in nature. (lower right)

# Nevada City Cohousing
# Nevada City, California

## Seniors in Intergenerational Cohousing

Some seniors find the youthful vigor of a mixed-generational cohousing community to be refreshing. They enjoy the hustle and bustle of children and the energy for life they generate. We have shown examples of senior cohousing communities that are adjacent to intergenerational communities, such as Munksøgård and Silver Sage. In practice, they complement each other. In fact, cohousing communities founded a generation ago in Denmark are now being retrofitted to better meet the changing needs of their many residents who have grown older.

In traditional cohousing, communities tend to focus on children, young families, and the concerns of mid-adult life. But some larger cohousing communities, such as Nevada City Cohousing, have enough seniors to accommodate the interests and needs of the older residents.

Thirty-four households moved into Nevada City Cohousing in 2006, among them twenty seniors and as many children. The older members have plenty of opportunities to enjoy community with their peers. They can also partake in common dinners held six nights a week, and have their choice of the many community-wide amenities and activities that a large community with a diversity of ages and interests can offer.

**Same Page, Top:** Senior residents at Nevada City Cohousing can easily visit each other and enjoy time outdoors.

**Bottom**: Nira is delighted by a birthday cake in the common house and the company of her neighbors.

I asked 92-year-old Meg, who lives in Nevada City Cohousing, why she moved from a house right next to the parking lot to a house located about 700 feet from the parking lot. She said that the relationships with her neighbors are a lot more important to her than her relationship with her car. Meg lived there until she was 97.

Nevada City Cohousing, a 34-unit intergenerational community, was built in 2005 in a beautiful rural setting at the edge of a small but vibrant town in the Sierra Nevada foothills.

Residents are only a short walk from downtown cafes, restaurants, shops, theaters, and a farmers' market.

# Part 5
# New Projects and Communities in Design

## Senior Cohousing, Timeless and Progressive

People want to believe that cohousing is a new and exotic experiment. To the contrary, the concept of cohousing is timeless and basic. Humans have always needed meaningful social interactions, a feeling of connectedness. In a word, community.

Over the last few years, McCamant & Durrett Architects (MDA) has created some of the most progressive, yet timeless, senior cohousing communities anywhere. In Port Townsend, Washington, a group of seniors workshopped their way to a custom neighborhood that now accommodates their needs and desires. In Mountain View, California, nineteen households came together to build a small village in the middle of a sprawling metro area. In Stillwater, Oklahoma, a dynamic senior duo were the driving force that built a functioning community within a suburban subdivision, affordably. In Vancouver, British Columbia, a group of individuals joined forces to build a senior- and child-friendly community that has become an anchor of their urban neighborhood. In Chilliwack, British Columbia, a former dairy farm is being transformed into a commercial and cultural center, with cohousing at its core.

Seniors are busy creating new cohousing communities. In Shepherdstown, West Virginia, a group of seniors are creating a community where they will live with dignity and gusto in their culturally creative college town. In Santa Cruz, California, a group of seniors are downsizing with great intent so that they may enjoy the riches of city life together. In Fair Oaks, California, a mix of seniors

and young families are creating an eco-forward neighborhood that will fit them like a glove. In Durham, North Carolina, a group of LGBT seniors is creating a village where they can age actively among friends and allies in an environment that is supporting and genuine.

The cohousing concept is also influencing other senior housing projects in astonishing and innovative ways. In a rural setting near Auburn (Nevada County), California, a small town will someday invite seniors to age successfully in community by simply stepping out their front door. In American Canyon, California, in southern Napa County, a nonprofit affordable housing project will provide both homes and community for low-income seniors. And around the United States, Opportunity Villages offer a viable and innovative solution to the problems of homelessness.

As impressive as these projects are, the fact is that people who create cohousing are everyday folks. They are physical therapists, school teachers, and techies. They are engaged citizens who simply want to improve their community. They could be your friends, your neighbors, your family, yourself.

If you can see yourself living in a cohousing community, then the truth is you can. Over the next pages, you'll see where others have already ne. Let them amaze you. Let them inspire you. Let them show you the way home.

Senior Cohousing Primer—Recent Examples + New Projects

## Port Townsend, Washington
## Quimper Village

Growing older? Want to talk? Those were the questions posed to advertise a meeting on a January afternoon at the local church. Sixty-five seniors showed up. Pat and David Hundhausen, the organizers, gave about a half-hour introduction, talking about their quest to get out of denial about aging, apprehensions about typical aging scenarios, and an alternative scenario in which new friends could live together in their own small homes in a small supportive community that they helped design and would manage themselves.

"We're getting older, and lucky to do so. We want to set ourselves up for success," they said.

They introduced a new development concept, senior cohousing, that they hoped to bring to Port Townsend, and then they announced the activity for the afternoon—to break up into ten groups of about six people each and take 45 minutes to have a conversation: How do we grow older successfully? How do we set ourselves up for

**FACING PAGE, CLOCKWISE FROM TOP LEFT:**

Cohousing is about people getting to know each other before the first block is laid. It takes a community to make a community. People who share a history together have a story. There is no place better to grow that story than the creative, personal, and community-building experience of designing cohousing together.

This drawing was inspired by my association with England, a place with less than one hundred sunny days a year. One of my elder relatives there would always take refuge in a greenhouse when drizzle turned to rain. In cohousing, a greenhouse can be a common place where neighbors can pot plants or have a cup of tea with one another when the weather turns gray.

In a place as gray as Port Townsend, which has only about one hundred sixty sunny days a year, you must bring color to the buildings to brighten those moody days.

Senior Cohousing Primer—Recent Examples + New Projects  **68**

success? What is our emerging reality? Who do we do it with, and what does it look like?

Afterward, they met together again so that each group could share its responses. A representative of each group was asked to present keywords that came out of their group. But there was a catch: Speakers would present one at a time, and subsequent speakers were asked not to repeat keywords. The last group had no new words; there was that much overlap. The keywords included: "Independence; Community; Friends nearby; Live lighter on the planet."

Pat and David then wound up the meeting describing the next step they were organizing, the SG1 Aging Successfully Workshop. At each table was a sign-up sheet for participants who wanted to carry on the conversation further at a later date. Forty people signed up.

From this workshop, five households proceeded with developing a custom neighborhood they envisioned and planned, based on what they thought would be responsive to their needs, wants, and desires—a cohousing community for seniors. Folks who considered joining later asked that the SG1 Workshop be repeated so they would have the same foundation.

### FACING PAGE, TOP:

Designed to capture the southern sun, cohousing facilitates a sense of place and community long after the honeymoon has worn off. This site design breathes life into a neighborhood, where walking or wheeling (but not driving) past familiar neighbors and extending warm salutations or a helping hand create longtime and meaningful relationships.

### BOTTOM:

A group creates meaning by talking and writing and planning together with intention. Just observe the intensity of their site design process. No traditional developer would ever, could ever, create a site plan like this. The focus of the discussion is to create a site plan that is pedestrian friendly.

→ Site Plan

"You cannot make a decision to take action ten minutes before going into a corporate aging facility."

— *Pat Hundhausen, resident of Quimper Village*

**FACING PAGE:**

The common house is an extension of the private homes. With the 5,000 square feet of common facilities and your own 920-square-foot house, every resident has nearly 6,000 square feet of living space. Add a caretaker suite, and you and your neighbors have something much more important than real estate.

Quimper Village residents together created goals, activities, and places to ensure that the common house would be a safe and fun place for everyone. Their goals were to manifest their community, a community that was beautiful, comfortable, and welcoming. They wanted to use the common house to relax, dance, and play music. The group also agreed that a kitchen, dining room, and caretaker unit were places within the common space that made their goals and activities possible.

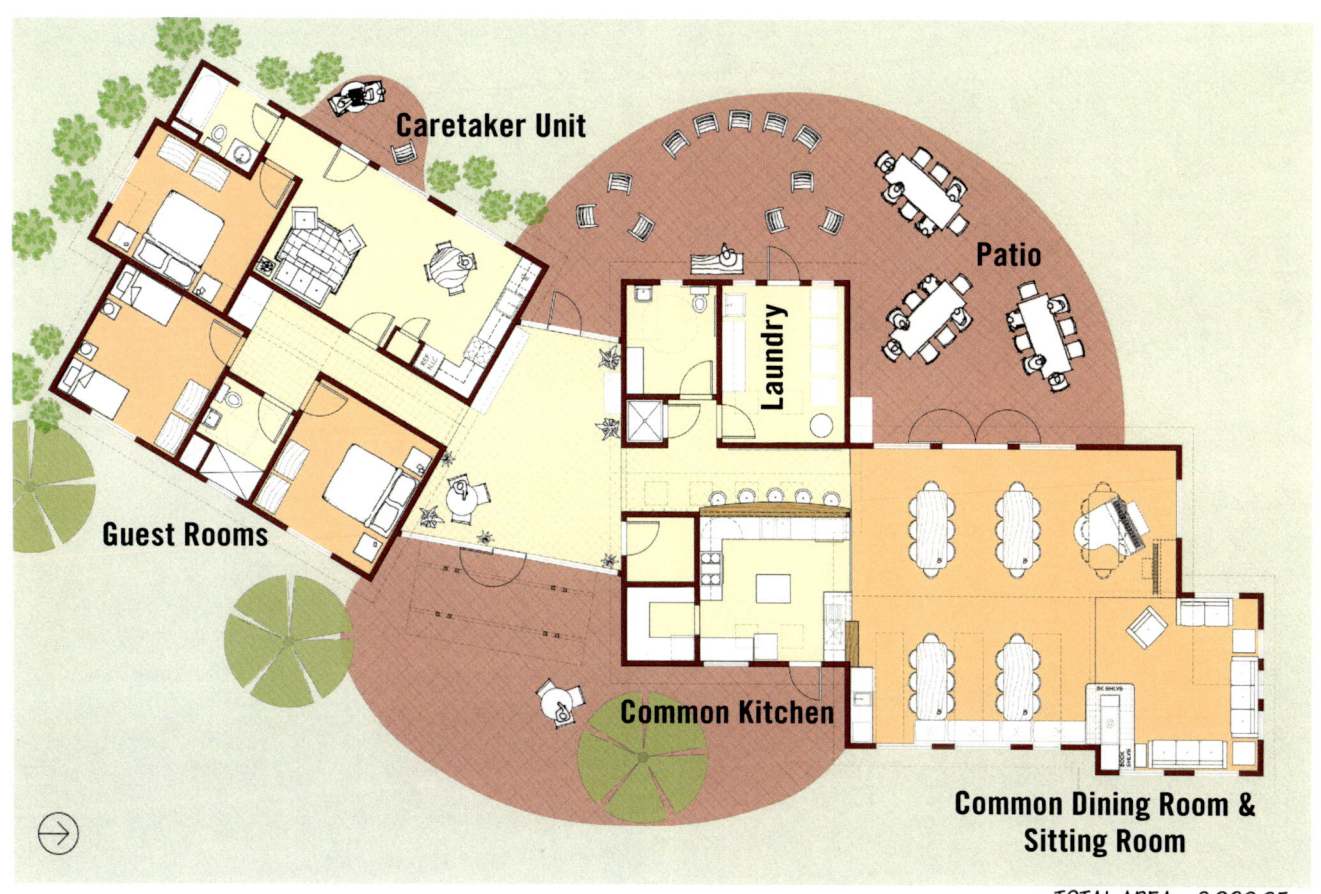

TOTAL AREA = 2,960 SF

Senior Cohousing Primer—Recent Examples + New Projects

**FACING PAGE AND NEXT PAGE (SPREAD):**

A village—why not? Cohousing is where the architecture serves the purpose of reinforcing the stated goals of the residents. Quimper Village reminds me of villages that I have seen in Southern France and in the rural, mountainous regions of Italy and America. It reminds me of the villages that I worked near in Africa. Timeless places that evolved organically over centuries. This site plan took a weekend, not centuries, to realize. My conclusion is that it takes centuries or a collective vision to design a village.

**SAME PAGE:**

The Quimper Village group enjoys spending time with their neighbors, breaking bread together and hanging out in the common house, talking about the goings on of the day.

Photo credits: Quimper Village

Quimper Village Common Terrace. Architecture by McCamant & Durrett Architects.

## Mountain View, California
## Mountain View Cohousing

Nineteen houses and a 4,000-square-foot common house, all on 0.9 acres. "But we don't call it *senior* cohousing, just cohousing," the residents insisted. They are the first to admit that they are not completely out of denial about the realities of aging, at least not yet. MDA led all six Design Workshops, created the designs with the group, and developed the design drawings, and then represented the group during the city approval hearings. The group hired a development partner, who acquired construction financing, and built the project. A local architect finished the last 20 percent of the working drawings and specifications. This project began what is now our favored implementation process—working with local architects.

Drawings and details, developed during the one of the workshops led by MDA, gave the group a good look at how their project could feel—its essence. We continued to work with the group during the construction of their

**FACING PAGE, CLOCKWISE FROM TOP LEFT:**

Marsha came to cohousing because of her spouse. Now, she is an active committee member in her community. One spouse is often more in the game than the other, but after move-in you can't guess which one. Katie McCamant (CoHousing Solutions) contends that most people, if just dropped into cohousing, would more than thrive; they'd love it.

Single-family homes can feel isolating, even in town, especially for seniors. Cohousing communities that are built on an urban lot factor in the access to a pedestrian-friendly downtown and public transportation. This model of land use is often talked about in theory, but cohousing groups have accomplished it project after project.

Future residents of Mountain View Cohousing reviewing comments during the Common House Design Workshop. After they spent two full days creating a design criteria, we came back with a design for them to evaluate in groups. We guided them through the process, as needed.

Senior Cohousing Primer—Recent Examples + New Projects  **78**

community, choosing options that would keep energy costs and maintenance to a minimum. From previous experience, we knew how to save the group money and include architectural details the group would care about once they moved in.

The United Nations' World Habitat Award, which MDA won and was presented with on United Nations World Habitat Day in 2001, is based on the notion that the American middle class consumes too much of the earth's resources. The U.N. perceived that cohousing was addressing that problem (as well as many others). In many ways, Mountain View Cohousing represents everything that we need to accomplish in our current housing crisis. It improves quality of life and uses fewer

> "... I go jogging with Jeff almost every day. It's easy—he just lives a few doors down."
>
> — *Joe, resident of Mountain View Cohousing*

**FACING PAGE:**

The 19-unit community sits on 0.9 acres on what was a single-family parcel. We moved the small white house to the street to allow for the best placement and most efficient building of the nineteen units. Moving a single-family house to a more useful location, or otherwise improving the utility of a lot, is essential in many cases when building a cohousing community on an urban setting.

In the case of Mountain View Cohousing, the "neighborhood" has the advantage of being a small village set in the middle of a city. The cohousing community has a large garden and common space, and retains walkability to the city center, which is one of the most pleasant central business districts in California.

resources than average upper middle class houses do. Cohousing also empowers people to get out of homes that no longer serve them and into a supportive old-world village-like setting.

Katie and I visited the group fourteen months after move-in. Still thrilled by what they created, the memories, and the common history shaped from working together to get the project designed and approved, the camaraderie was palpable. The resident dynamics reminded me of a sports team that had just won the national championship and were now at the neighborhood

**FACING PAGE, CLOCKWISE FROM LEFT:**

Mountain View Cohousing has nineteen dwelling units, an elaborate caretaker unit, and a large common house on 0.9 acres. The only way to accomplish this was to put the parking entirely underground. There is no residual space on this site plan—every square foot was crafted with the kind of strategic open space allocation that makes the site feel gracious and open.

Neighbors being neighborly in a private outdoor space.

Common meals are at the heart of Mountain View Cohousing.

**SAME PAGE:**

Lifestyle sketches (created after the design workshops) articulate the intended lifestyle in the community. These drawings help the group, the neighbors, friends and family, and the city officials imagine the lifestyles and behavior that the group intends to foster.

Senior Cohousing Primer—Recent Examples + New Projects

**FACING PAGE:**

Making a three-story building with a full basement (for underground parking) not feel too bulky in a single-family neighborhood is always a challenge. To do that, you have to gift it something—a warm and giving façade often does the trick. Neighbors will better appreciate the structure if the warmth of the design is obvious from the street.

Reminiscent of villages, and of cohousing everywhere, there is an obvious life between the buildings. This is the point. In cohousing, it's not hard to notice that people know, care about, and support one another.

**SAME PAGE:**

Open-air walkways are natural meeting places, where people can have a cup of tea and talk about issues of today or plan their shopping date for tomorrow.

**NEXT PAGE (SPREAD):**

Mountain View Cohousing elevation sketch, a beautifully detailed framework for seniors to have fun and age successfully.

**Senior Cohousing Primer—Recent Examples + New Projects**

pub after the big game. It was great testimony as to why groups must be an integral part of the organizing, planning, and design. This is how the community is built—the only way.

There are stories aplenty that come out of this group, but one is particularly noteworthy: "Joe," I asked, "how the heck did you get into such great physical shape since I last saw you?" Being previously much heavier, he explained, "Well, living here now, I go jogging with Jeff [his neighbor in cohousing] almost every day." Astounded, I rejoined, "Every day?" Joe replied, "It's easy—he just lives a few doors down."

One of the most effective tools for getting seniors into a proactive mindset is Study Group 1 Aging Successfully (SG1). SG1 comprises a series of ten sessions, and each of these sessions is often facilitated by one of the group's very own members. The objective of these sessions is to bring up some of the not-so-comfortable questions and fears about aging so that participants will talk through them. Through these discussions seniors discover the issues of aging, and then decide how to reach out and grasp them. The result is a group that has both feet pointed to the future—ready to be an active part of their own successful aging.

Currently, it is estimated that about 40 percent of participants of an SG1 Workshop will choose to pursue cohousing as a housing choice—a promising number, but still a number to improve upon. You can learn more about SG1 in The Senior Cohousing Handbook: A Community Approach to Independent Living (New Society Publishers) or by visiting SAGECohousingInternational.org.

To find out about our online facilitator training, visit www.cohousingco.com/study-group-1.

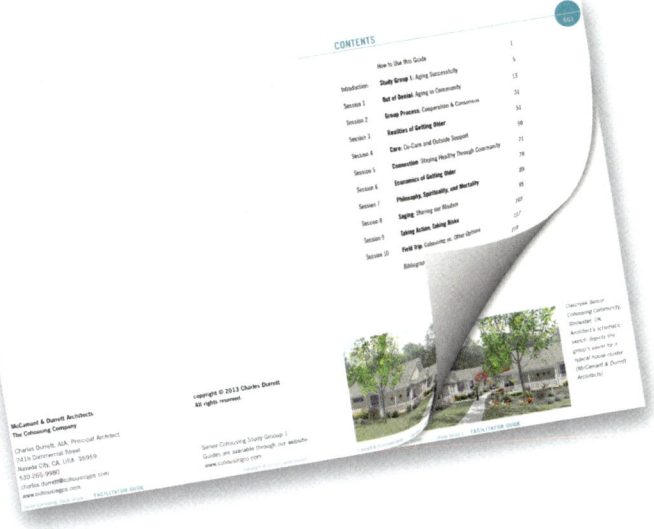

The SG1 Workshop Guides are filled with exercises for you that help seniors become aware of the issues, get out of denial, and get into supportive housing. Become a facilitator and help groups around you get started. More information at www.cohousingco.com

Senior Cohousing Primer—Recent Examples + New Projects 88

## Stillwater, Oklahoma
## Oakcreek Community

Yes, Study Group 1 is how individuals can clarify the realities of aging. And yes, a vibrant senior cohousing group can emerge from individuals who engage in that work together. But a senior cohousing community can also be created by a couple of people who are good leaders and a number of other people who are smart enough to see what's happening and jump on board. In this case, one of those visionary leaders was Pat Darlington who, after attending a week-long SG1 Facilitator Training in Boulder, Colorado, stepped up to the plate. She and Kay Stewart provided the leadership (they would come to be known as the Thelma & Louise of their project), and they sponsored Katie and Chuck to facilitate a Getting-It-Built (G.I.B.) Workshop in Stillwater, Oklahoma. The rest of the group followed because they had compassionate (and smart) leaders.

**FACING PAGE, CLOCKWISE FROM TOP LEFT:**

Future residents critiquing the common house after two days of generating design criteria. This kind of care ensures that the common house will see 300–400 people hours per week. Without this participation, the common house would be used fewer than 100 people hours per week.

People often ask, "Chuck, you've done this many times. Why don't you just design the site plan?" My feeling is that real people bring real experiences and real values to the table. My job is to make sure they don't miss any opportunities or make mistakes. It's a much better design with their participation.

The drawings explain the design. They are more than just illustrations—the future residents must see and believe in the realities that the drawings represent. And that makes it a lot easier to get approval from the city.

Senior Cohousing Primer—Recent Examples + New Projects

> "We're not driving off a cliff, because we discovered a means of providing for ourselves, of living better by learning to cooperate. We discovered cohousing."
>
> — Pat Darlington

The group wanted to construct an entire neighborhood that was designed to shelter them from the annual tornadoes that sweep through Oklahoma. But they also wanted to live in a neighborhood where they could have tea with their neighbors and talk about the issues of the day (whether to get knee surgery or not, where to view the wild flowers, and who's driving to the movies). They wanted to wrap the buildings around the reality they wanted, not the other way around. And so they decided to bend their living environment and impose their will on it.

MDA was asked to design six of twenty-four brand-new houses that cost no more than $150,000 each. All future residents were clear that they did not want to grow old

**FACING PAGE:**

Seniors enjoying the common house that they helped create. It is a building that not only fulfills their needs, wants, and desires (individually and collectively) but also fulfills who they aspire to be. In other words, the common house makes life more economical, practical, convenient, healthy, interesting, and fun.

**BELOW:**

The group works together to design the common house that works for everyone.

like their parents had, denying the realities of aging and suffering the consequences. All were clear that they wanted to live in a loving, supportive, high-functioning neighborhood where they knew, grew to care about, and, by extension, could readily support each other. They understood that proximity makes a big difference for aging successfully.

To kick off the project, Pat and Kay bought a single-family house on an oversized lot in one of the most expensive neighborhoods in town. They believed there was a better use for the site than a single house. But in order to build their community they would have to get this property rezoned to twenty-four units. No small feat. But they got it done.

Working to build an innovative housing project like this was an education for its future residents. They learned how to listen to their neighbors, how to consider the issues of the day within the context of their larger community, and how to transform the dream of their project into a reality. Moreover, during the process of creating

**FACING PAGE, TOP LEFT AND RIGHT:**

From drawing board to reality. The drawings that explained the design remain a reference point for residents as they see the buildings take form during construction and as they move in to their new community.

**BOTTOM LEFT AND RIGHT:**

Seniors do a great job of maintaining their own property and delegating tasks among themselves. In Nevada City Cohousing, 97-year old Meg (not shown here) was a great cheerleader from her electric wheelchair. When in community, you become inspired to create something beautiful, and working with others is a lot more fun than gardening alone in your backyard.

Photo credits: Oakcreek Community

cohousing, more than a few residents kindled a desire to make a positive difference in a bigger way. Ever the leader, Pat Darlington joined the city council in Stillwater after moving into Oakcreek Community. Today she is an active participant in the business of both her neighborhood and city.

Oakcreek Community is the reason that Thelma & Louise did not drive off a cliff. Oakcreek Community is not only why its residents continue to lead productive lives but also why they continue to grow in leaps and bounds. On their website, they declare that they are neighbors enjoying a neighborhood, a neighborhood with lots of open green space where they see their neighbors more than they see their cars and know their neighbors by name and who they can contact should they have an emergency.

**FACING PAGE, TOP:**

There are always grandkids at this senior cohousing community and everybody loves it. In cohousing, seniors have as much fun and meaning in the next fifty years of their lives as they did in their first fifty.

**FAR RIGHT:**

Warm, inviting front porches.

**BOTTOM:**

Being together, eldering each other, talking about issues of the day, sharing stories. These are important components of growing older successfully, components of successful retirement and elderhood. The conversations in senior cohousing go deeper, even becoming philosophical, over time.

Photo credits: Oakcreek Community and Margaret Roesch

Senior Cohousing Primer—Recent Examples + New Projects

## Shepherdstown, West Virginia
## Shepherd Village

In September 2015, MDA met with a group of twenty-eight older adults to facilitate a Site Design Workshop in Shepherdstown, a small college town with about 1,700 people. This community has a rich variety of residents, from young children to older adults and students. On a 19-acre site within walking distance of the historic downtown and Shepherd University, the cohousing group was working to create a thirty-unit senior community for themselves.

The future residents of Shepherd Village continue to stay creative and healthy in the their community of Shepherdstown. They enjoy cultural and historic events, and they are active walkers and bird watchers. They have pride in Shepherdstown and want to age gracefully in it. As they get older, however, they understand that they will need the support of others. What better way to be happy, inspired, and have fun, than by cultivating a place with others with a shared vision!

**FACING PAGE, CLOCKWISE FROM TOP LEFT:**

The participatory process for the site design results in the creation of a neighborhood that is based on relationships (running into neighbors) and health (walking).

Community members discuss how the design will accomplish their intended goals, activities, and desired neighborly behaviors.

The group is clearly appreciative of what they've done together, creating their new village. The participatory process helps these future neighbors get in touch with their own values and culture, and what they want their lives to be about in the future.

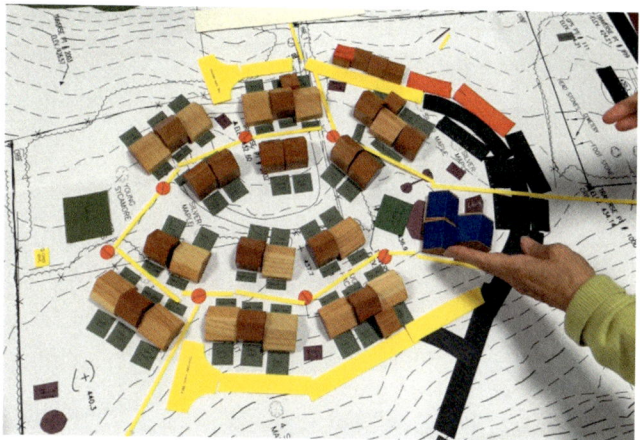

Senior Cohousing Primer—Recent Examples + New Projects

The Shepherd Village group had a wonderful site and a strong commitment to their stated principles. Our role as facilitators was to help them focus their vision, and help them recognize the practical value of their assets and transform their desires into a tangible reality. Together, we worked to use our time effectively and to keep the project moving forward. As a result, we brought closure to the many stages of the process, including the site, common house, and private house designs. The group moved through material selection quickly, having a solid vision for their small, supportive community. The entire process took only a couple of months.

The group continues to explore and build their cohousing community with a local architect, who came to the design workshops and read The Senior Cohousing Handbook: A Community Approach to Independent Living so he could work effectively with the group. The challenge the group has moving forward is to keep the momentum they had in the workshops, which is made a lot easier with a seasoned cohousing architect. When we hand off the baton to someone else (a rare occurrence), we require that he or she knows how to work with the

> College-based alumni senior cohousing is a trend in retirement communities for active adults. It allows retiring alumni to engage in a life-long exchange with their alma mater that significantly enhances the college community and the quality of life in higher learning institutions. This is a beneficial exchange for students, alumni, their families and friends, and ultimately for society at large. Contact MDA for more information on creating a college-based alumni senior cohousing in your community.

**FACING PAGE:**

Although this appears to be an ideal senior cohousing site plan, in truth it is only one particular group's version of what "ideal" is. The group next door will have a different version as they take into consideration site characteristics, terrain, angle of the sun, budget, and their own personal desires.

project group. Without this connection, cohousing communities are vulnerable to losing momentum, or once built, to be lacking in community.

Shepherd Village, when created, will be at the leading edge of creating senior cohousing in close proximity to a university or college. MDA has been approached by university leaders in Shepherdstown and in Stillwater, Oklahoma, and are exploring the possibility of working with higher learning centers to create cohousing for alumni, within or next to campus, availing opportunities for seniors to learn and contribute to the campus community. We see this as a benefit for schools and for alumni to build stronger, more supportive relationships for generations to come.

**FACING PAGE:**

In cohousing, nature mixed with village homes creates a sense of being in another time, but with the conveniences of our modern era. Cohousing design—village design—is timeless, regardless of any technological advances.

## Shepherd Village vision statement

"We are people who have lived vibrantly and meaningfully, worked for what we believe in, raised families, engaged with our communities and circles of connection, invested our talents and resources wholeheartedly.

"As we age, we want to continue celebrating the gift of life and joyfully engage with each other.

"However, as older adults, we need housing options that reflect our emerging needs as well as our values.

"We want to live more simply now, in homes that will support our independence as we become less mobile, and in a neighborhood that keeps us engaged with each other and the community.

## Santa Cruz, California
## Walnut Commons

What started out as an intergenerational cohousing project, ended up as a senior cohousing community. Located smack in the middle of the busiest part of town, Walnut Commons uses downtown Santa Cruz as a natural extension of their community. It's important to note that members of this group wanted to downsize from their sprawling suburban and rural lifestyles so they could enjoy the compact conveniences of an urban environment. They gave up acreage, and more acreage, in favor of *poquito magnifico*—small and beautiful. They were able to successfully accomplish this in large part because they created cohousing.

With a park nearby, easy access to public transportation, and ten espresso machines within a two-block radius, they are set up to enjoy an interesting, fun, and urban lifestyle.

From a community perspective, Walnut Commons presented an interesting design challenge. The site is small

**FACING PAGE, TOP:**

Although the Walnut Commons site is only 0.24 acres, we still approached the Site Design Workshop as we would with any other. But instead of using blocks, we used flat pieces of colored paper to represent apartments, hallways, the common house, gathering nodes, private decks, and the common terrace. Again, the residents turned out to be the best co-design partners and co-architects that we could have asked for.

In the Site Design Workshop the residents discussed what they wanted the common corridor to feel like and how they would actually use it if we designed it right.

When properly facilitated, the future residents can clearly see how the design of a given space (one foot narrower or wider) will affect their behavior for decades to come.

**BOTTOM:**

Meals shared with each other, and with guests, are a timeless way to strengthen and solidify community.

(0.24 acres), and the individual residences and common facilities are contained in a single, multilevel building. The challenge was to design a vertical environment that facilitated natural, casual neighborly interaction. Many people, including this group, found they are better able to circulate and connect when their setting has a horizontal orientation. People relate to each other horizontally, eye to eye. In terms of cohousing, this is usually facilitated with one- and two-story homes set along a walkway that links each home.

But cohousing can be successfully built in a vertical environment. At Walnut Commons, the common parking is underground. The vertical circulation areas (stairs, elevator) are located right in the middle of the structure, and are designed to bring people into the common areas. When going home (be it on the first, second, or third floors) most people stop on the first floor to get their mail, to check their laundry, to remind themselves what's for common dinner, or to prep the guest rooms for their guests. There are common facilities on each floor. The second floor has the open-air deck with the hot tub, perfect for stargazing. The third floor has the view of the sunset. Even the roof is prepped for future improvements.

This design was a Rubik's Cube all the way and, because the residents participated in its creation, it turned out to be an extremely values-based habitat. Passersby are engaged as they peek into windows of the common house. Being able to see residents in their kitchens means that the heartbeat of the community is "felt" as you walk the wide (and furnished) corridors. The residents, who are party to that conversation, value the feel of this heartbeat.

**FACING PAGE, TOP:**

The front street façade, solar panels included. Reminiscent of California's craftsman mission architecture, it suits the essential three C's of cohousing architecture: culture, costs, and climate.

**BOTTOM:**

The commitment to success is realized in all the fun that residents have in the co-creation process.

Senior Cohousing Primer—Recent Examples + New Projects

## Fair Oaks, California
## Fair Oaks EcoHousing

Fair Oaks EcoHousing is designed to accommodate families and older adults. So how can you make something that "fits like a glove" for both seniors and children? It can be a challenge, but Fair Oaks EcoHousing proves that it is possible.

With the guidance of MDA and CoHousing Solutions, the group designed a site that facilitates activities for all ages. Located central to the private homes is a 3,800 square-foot club house, which will have a play area for kids and other multi-purpose rooms for tai-chi and other activities. Other common facilities include a pool and spa, green space, and a workshop. The resident group planned for the diversity that they hope to achieve.

Early on, future residents of Fair Oaks EcoHousing participated in a Getting-It-Built Workshop (G.I.B., see page 113) to established clear goals and to learn various management and legal structures. Most importantly, they

**FACING PAGE, CLOCKWISE FROM TOP:**

The sixth design workshop is the Prioritization Workshop (shown here). All six Design Workshops are interesting, but the Prioritization Workshop is perhaps the most provocative. It is here where the clear set of values of the group reveals itself.

On a site walk with the future residents. So often a cohousing group will look at a site and become discouraged. But a group will start to see all the potential that almost every bit of land holds when they work with someone who has a practiced eye.

The group co-designs how the community will lay out in the Site Design Workshop. This workshop is critical because the result lays the foundation for how the community will live out their values, together.

Senior Cohousing Primer—Recent Examples + New Projects  **108**

learned how to work together as a team to co-create the cohousing neighborhood of their dreams.

From the beginning, residents of Fair Oaks EcoHousing stated that being light on the environment was a primary value shared amongst the group. Their design was endorsed by the Environmental Council of Sacramento in 2017 and 2018. The group proves that, with patience, perseverance, and a clear vision you can make the world a better place.

**FACING PAGE:**

Fair Oaks EcoHousing common house.

**BELOW:**

The Fair Oaks EcoHousing group broke ground in November 2017.

Fair Oaks EcoHousing continues to broaden its reach. In an effort to gather more members, the group writes news releases, tabled at local events, and go door-to-door to local schools and businesses with flyers. The hard work this group has put in has paid off—they've been featured in *Sacramento Parent*, *American River Messenger*, and *Sacramento Bee*.

Fair Oaks EcoHousing broke ground in November 2017 and it is already a successful community because its members have worked closely together, learned how to solve big questions, and are not afraid to change their minds or their designs if it benefits their community. This project ensures sustainability through its environmental choices and through co-design because they have chosen to live in a village of smaller than average houses with larger than average opportunities to cooperate. They relate in a healthier, more neighborly way to each other and, in doing so, they drive less, consume less, and give much more as a natural extension of the culture they've helped to create.

**ABOVE:**

Making pizza together. (Credit: Fair Oaks EcoHousing)

**FACING PAGE:**

State-of-the-art Fair Oaks EcoHousing Site Plan. The community is designed to cater to families of various sizes and individuals. Houses range from one to four bedrooms. All residents have full access to the common house, adding another 3,800 square feet to their living space!

Senior Cohousing Primer—Recent Examples + New Projects 112

The **Getting-It-Built Workshop (G.I.B.)** is designed to establish the vision and a plan for a cohousing group. During the two-day workshop, participants learn how to organize a strong group and work together. Groups can do this workshop with or without a site; however, the advantage of having a site is looking at feasibility and starting to think about costs. In any case, the G.I.B. walks participants through the financial and management options, including how to stay on budget.

The G.I.B. is one of the biggest indicators of the success of a cohousing project. Participants range from committed members to prospects to professionals who want to learn how to help groups create cohousing (i.e., architects, developers, etc.), and all benefit greatly from the experience. The workshop is co-facilitated by CoHousing Solutions and MDA.

**FACING PAGE:**

Fair Oaks EcoHousing hired MDA and CoHousing Solutions to facilitate the G.I.B. before they began designing their community. This workshop helps groups to plan for their future cohousing community by establishing a vision for the group. The next step are the Design Workshops where future residents create the look and feel of their project.

Senior Cohousing Primer—Recent Examples + New Projects 114

## Vancouver, British Columbia
## Vancouver Cohousing

Vancouver Cohousing is a great example of seniors joining forces with the youth to get their project built. This is a project initiated by twenty and thirty-year-olds, hand-in-hand with the sixty and seventy-year-olds. Affordability is tough in Vancouver, where the average urban house in 2010 cost $778,000. Rezoning the property and deciding on shared houses and smaller house plans (as small as 450 square feet) saved the group more than $100,000 per house. This was possible in large part because the group decided on a generous 6,000-square-foot common house.

Yonas Jongkind and I went to Vancouver on five different occasions to find a site for the group. They made several failed offers before developer Alan Forrester said, "I think I have just the site for you." All that remained was getting the site designed and then rezoning the site.

The biggest challenge was that the group needed to have the faith that the site would be rezoned (and they did). They knew that the design they created was compelling and sensitive. In the meantime, the community strengthened, workshop after workshop, not only through the design efforts but with the exhaustive strategic work necessary to secure the rezoning. The process itself empowered the community to engage with the city to get the needed approvals.

Vancouver Cohousing is known throughout Canada as urban development done right. The mayor has visited numerous times, asking the group how they created such a vibrant and interesting community. How did they manage to create what so many seasoned developers said that they wanted to create, but never could?

**FACING PAGE:**

I worked with the group on the site plan during the Site Design Workshop and with the residents who wanted a two-bedroom, one-bath design during the Private House Design Workshop. These workshops are where residents work together and bring their dream to life through beautiful architectural renderings.

How is it possible that these neophyte developers (physical therapists, school teachers, and techies) could do what a forty-year veteran developer could not? The answer is simple—the group's creative problem-solving exceeded the potential of the veteran developer just looking in the rearview mirror asking himself what sold last time. Instead, the group asked, Where do we want to be and how do we get there? They employed cohousing math (one plus one is three) with every decision—I have an idea, you have an idea, and the idea that we come up with together is better than either of the others. The group came up with great ideas, one after another, until it became clear that Vancouver Cohousing was going to be both senior- and child-friendly (in other words, all-age friendly).

Many single parents came to the table with concerns. "Will my son have friends his age?" "Will Grandma be alone when she visits and we are at work?" Their concerns came from previous experience—the norm in many cases—where the architecture does not facilitate a functioning society.

**FACING PAGE:**
Early drawings of Vancouver Cohousing are used to get the site rezoned from three single family houses to thirty-one dwelling units. The site is on a major public transit corridor, next to a fledgling neighborhood center. The new cohousing residents, now creating a larger community, will help support both the public transit and neighborhood center.

The neighbors resisted the project at first but, as is too often the case, once it was built they came to appreciate the renewed stability of the bus route and local stores. Mostly, they appreciate that the cohousing group organized their community in the best interest of the entire neighborhood. Vancouver Cohousing offers cooking classes and gardening seminars, eldering neighborhood-wide. This cohousing community is a huge shot in the arm for the surrounding neighborhood.

Senior Cohousing Primer—Recent Examples + New Projects  **118**

The city officials impeded a smooth approval process, however. Their requests presented the group with unnecessary costs and, even worse, were deleterious to the community: "Just add one more thing." "Turn the front door this way." "Turn the back door that way." "Put another set of stairs on the front of the building. Now put another set of stairs on the front."

Delay after delay, expense after expense, the group persevered. Bureaucrats drew comparisons of this project with Brand X—developments that failed before (but were not cohousing) and in doing so, couldn't see that this group was different. In the end, however, the support and positive responses from future residents made the city recognize that they had unnecessarily encumbered the process. It's worth noting that a subsequent cohousing community in Vancouver took much less time and money to create.

**FACING PAGE:**

Vancouver Cohousing, completed in 2016, is already a vital part of the neighborhood.

**BELOW:**

The future residents of Vancouver Cohousing worked diligently to figure out the best use of the common facilities—the design that would encourage people to spend time there.

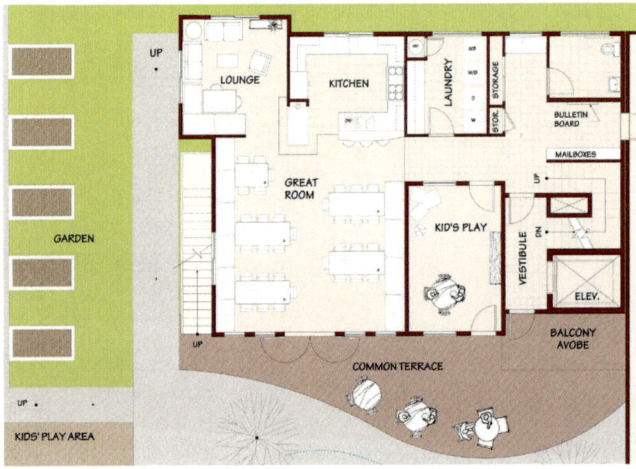

## Chilliwack, British Columbia
## Yarrow Ecovillage

Started by eighty-three-year-old Gerry, this project began with one big focus: living lighter on the planet. It turns out that fostering, creating, and implementing a cohousing community would best facilitate this vision. In fact, it goes without saying that living lighter on the planet involves cooperation, sharing, and trust—the basic tenets of cohousing.

Following the first cohousing community in the United States (Muir Commons in Davis, California) cohousing has not only continued to expand throughout the U.S. and Canada, it has also become a model for other housing types (senior housing and nonprofit affordable housing, for example). Cohousing is a building block for other larger communities—ecovillages in particular. The Yarrow Ecovillage in Chilliwack, British Columbia, is one such project. True to the cohousing concept, it aims to re-establish many of the advantages of traditional villages within the context of twenty-first century living.

**FACING PAGE, LEFT:**

Using cohousing creation methodologies, perfected by anthropologists in Denmark, this group is one of three resident groups who are separately prioritizing common house expenditures. Given their goals for community, common and personal convenience, and sustainability, to name a few, their desire for shared facilities was extensive and had to be prioritized.

Budget dictates that the large list of line items be prioritized down to fifteen items in Yarrow Ecovillage. This brings up an interesting exercise common to all cohousing groups: To further facilitate economy, they ask, can we increase the number of common amenities and make the private homes smaller? Sharing (common facilities) is one of the best ways to create a more convenient, practical, more economical community.

**RIGHT:**

The site plan, including multi-use and commercial space (upper), a future senior cohousing cluster, and 20 acres of community farmland (lower).

The site of this community is a former dairy farm, vacant since the 1980s. Quite conveniently, the site is on Yarrow Central Road, the main road that connects the town of Yarrow (drained by decades of suburban sprawl and now incorporated with Chilliwack) with urban Vancouver (to its west) and the natural beauty of the Fraser Valley.

Yarrow Ecovillage offers the possibility of creating a new town center for Yarrow, a place for living combined with commerce. The 25-acre site includes a 33-unit intergenerational cohousing community, plans for a seventeen-unit senior cohousing community, a 30,000-square-foot mixed-use area (commercial, rental units, learning center, farmers' market, etc.), and a 20-acre organic farm.

The concept of the town center is almost as old as human settlement. Members of Yarrow Ecovillage understand that the combination of positive, usable public space, combined with commercial activity and spaces for creativity and learning (their town center), activate the environment.

Such public space doesn't just provide retail opportunities; it also provides opportunities for meaningful human interaction. Over time, these spontaneous, informal interactions grow into more formal friendships. You get to know the person who bakes your bread, grows your carrots, or relaxes in the public square on a sunny day, and he or she gets to know you and your children. The variety of relationships and diversity of people, skills, and interests will likely establish a vibrant culture of learning, doing, and being—as a functional, interrelated society.

Yarrow Ecovillage is designed to offer an exceptional combination of cohousing, sustainable living, and farmland preservation. It is a live/work community, a

**FACING PAGE, TOP:**
Yarrow Ecovillage Common House.

**BOTTOM:**
Residents enjoy time together in many forms.

> The sixth design workshop, the Prioritization Workshop, is when fifteen to twenty-five amenities are put on the table and, in prioritizing them, you get to the kernel values of the individuals and then the values of the entire group. No righteousness, no guilt tripping, just genuine, heartfelt discussions and honest decisions.
>
> By contrast, developers who build houses on speculation install amenities using guesswork. They follow past market trends and default to high-gloss details like marble entryways and brass chandeliers in the hope they will facilitate a quick sale to an unknown buyer. Usually, cohousing groups choose instead to spend their money on amenities like extra insulation, solar panels, sustainably grown lumber, and better acoustics. They sometimes choose sexy countertops, too. Regardless, they choose what is important to them. I'm always amazed what a group of people decides is important once there is heartfelt and thoughtful conversation—usually marble entryways are the last thing that they are worried about.

learning center, and a mixed-use town center. Three main elements—living, working, and farming—along with many other activities and amenities such as learning, socializing, sharing, teaching, playing, and visiting, are designed to come together as a model for environmentally, economically, and socially sustainable lifestyles.

To accomplish the many objectives of the ecovillage, the city of Chilliwack worked with the cohousing group and its architects to establish an entirely new custom zoning code. The result is an "Ecovillage Zoning" designation that includes residential, commercial, cottage industries, work space, public open space, recreational space, and farming.

What the group has designed couldn't be more sophisticated—more synergistic. It has been likened to organic villages of old found in Southern France and elsewhere. Those villages were created before development became big box and big subdivision, when human environments were human scale.

That's Yarrow Ecovillage.

## Durham, North Carolina
## Village Hearth Cohousing

Cohousing is not a new concept in Durham. To date, there are three established cohousing communities in Durham, and many more in the broader scape of North Carolina. Village Hearth Cohousing will be the first LGBT senior cohousing community in the U.S. Sited on fifteen acres in North Durham, Village Hearth Cohousing seeks to be a model for a better, more supportive space for LGBT seniors and their allies. Quality, affordability, and conscious environmental design are key words to describe this project.

> "We want a community of shared history and understanding. People who know what I have been through. They are those that can best support me."
>
> —Pat McAulay

**FACING PAGE, CLOCKWISE FROM TOP LEFT:**

Katie McCamant (CoHousing Solutions) talking with the group about feasibility of their site. With a site, a cohousing group can more easily gather members because the costs are more tangible and the vision for design can begin.

Members of the group talk about how they can best work together to create the community of their dreams. These early meetings are key in creating a solid group dynamic.

Village Hearth Cohousing, a community of people who share a common history, have chosen cohousing as a way to ensure they can age safely and with others. (Pictured with MDA architects Gary Burke and myself).

Senior Cohousing Primer—Recent Examples + New Projects

In the case of Village Hearth, cohousing provides a place for people with a similar history to come together in support and solidarity. It makes sense that an LGBT community and their allies would want a village where they can be assured they are getting the best support possible, to live in community where supporting one another is an easy and genuine extension of one's self. For many in the LGBT senior community, a shared history is key, especially in a time when other options such as traditional senior communities, in-home care, and immediate families may be ineffective or even harmful.

Village Hearth Cohousing is working with MDA and CoHousing Solutions to create a sustainable path for their future, a future filled with fun and memories shared with people who know and trust each other. The group has already designed a stellar site plan and common house that encourages support, community. They are actively reaching out to senior organizations to grow their network and to show others that it is possible to create a safe community.

We are motivated to set up this group for success because cohousing is a tangible solution for the housing challenges of LGBT seniors. They have a lot of courage to do what they are doing, yet another quality inherent to those who pursue cohousing. Courage unsurprisingly moves projects forward with success.

**FACING PAGE, CLOCKWISE FROM TOP LEFT:**
The Village Hearth Cohousing group worked diligently through to create their future community. They co-designed a spectacular site plan (first image), a common house (second and third images), and private houses that fit their needs and desires. During the Design Closure Workshop (fourth image) the group saw their hard work come to life with colorful and detailed visual displays.

*The Future of LGBT Senior Housing*

On June 19, 2017, Village Hearth Cohousing was approved 7-0 by the Durham City Council and 14-0 by the Planning Commission. Durham, North Carolina has a vibrant LGBT culture and it is home to a few already established cohousing communities. If more cities could think like Durham, society as a whole would begin seeing positive shifts on several fronts, including housing and community.

Housing for LGBT adults is currently not safe and, in many places, non-existent. Some are even forced to comply with traditional gender roles (rather than preferred), putting them at greater risk of being persecuted and/or alone. Senior cohousing offers great advantages for LGBT adults with its intrinsic co-design, co-care characteristics. In senior cohousing, LGBTs are in a safe value-shared community.

**ABOVE:**

View along the pathway of the future Village Hearth Cohousing.

**FACING PAGE:**

Village Hearth will be the beginning of something new and exciting. It already has begun. Working together, the group co-designed a community that will be supportive, accepting, and fun. Working alongside cohousing consultants, the group will actualize their dreams and inspire a brighter future for other LGBT seniors.

# Nevada County, California
## Rincon del Rio

How would you define successful aging? Would you include factors such as health, safety, community, strong relationships, and contentment? Aging successfully is possible—even easy. All you need is to go back to basics of place, health, connectedness, and happiness. With this in mind, we helped to conduct a study within Nevada County that revealed two interesting conclusions: Local seniors want to stay in the region and they are not satisfied with current housing options. We worked alongside the property developers to design a solution for the challenge of housing seniors in the way they want to be housed in Nevada County, California.

Rincon del Rio is a pastoral setting of 215 acres on the Bear River, with verdant foliage, scenic vistas, ponds, and a serene atmosphere. Walking trails, contemplation areas, groomed, picturesque landscaping, and community gardens further complement the natural attributes. The buildings are clustered on the western 40 acres,

**FACING PAGE AND BELOW:**
Space for a stroll, parks, and tree-lined paths foster wellness for both younger and older people. Those who have easy access to large, attractive open space areas utilize them frequently. They are three times more likely to achieve recommended levels of physical activity and are 40 percent less likely to be overweight or obese as compared to people in less green settings.

preserving the natural beauty and ecosystems of the rest of the site.

Rincon del Rio's environment is its foundation. Officially a Continuing Care Retirement Community (CCRC) proposed in the gold country of Northern California, Rincon del Rio is a senior village near nature that supports physical activity and promotes healthy, successful aging. It is a compact, pedestrian-oriented, sustainable, and mixed-use neighborhood with local commercial services and three-hundred forty-five residential units built as a variety of small neighborhoods, including cohousing. Eighty percent of the site is dedicated open space, with recreation, trails, and community agriculture on a 25-acre working historic farm.

As part of a 2013 environmental impact report, results indicate that "Rincon del Rio will have a 60 percent smaller carbon footprint compared to average new developments." The reductions can be seen through many aspects of the CCRC: 60 percent less due to the use of alternative energy and energy efficiency (solar and

**FACING PAGE:**

Many new projects around the U.S., such as Rincon del Rio, are leveraging a cohousing community to get the rest of their development approved. Meanwhile, the cohousing model influences the rest of the project: community development, neighborhood management, water conservation efforts, you name it. This project will be a much-needed shot in the arm to Nevada County's economy, and the cohousing component will ensure that it's not "growth as usual" (in other words, not sprawl).

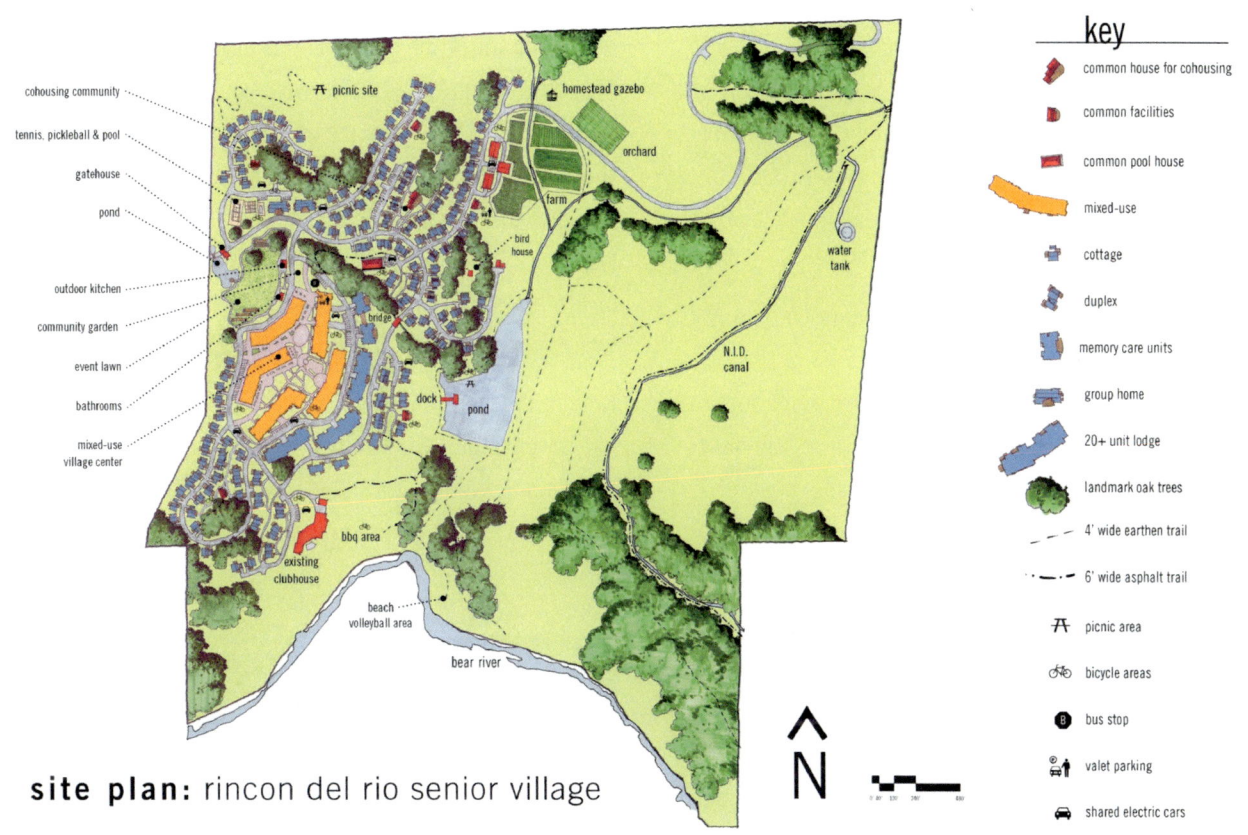

**site plan:** rincon del rio senior village

quality insulation, as examples); 55 percent less through designing a pedestrian-friendly community, with electric shuttle and carpooling services; 60 percent less on-site gases through efficient appliances and no-gas lawn equipment; and 65 percent less water and waste through recycling, drought-tolerant native landscaping, and a water reclamation program.

Rincon del Rio includes a senior cohousing community, a neighborhood of twenty affordable units, near the community farm. At the core of the cohousing neighborhood is a 3,500-square-foot common house. Here, residents enjoy eating meals together (that they cook) several times each week and plan other activities to do together. The common kitchen, dining room, large terrace, and additional shared spaces that serve the entire cohousing neighborhood preclude the need for each household to have extra guest rooms, big dining rooms, and the like. For this reason, private houses can be an efficient, yet spacious home, even at 900 square feet.

The goal of Rincon del Rio is to provide a responsive community, and the best way to accomplish a responsive community is by providing choice. Each neighborhood has a walking initiative, specific recreational attractions, and standard amenities. In this way, we've designed unique environments that can attract new friends throughout the village and surrounding neighborhoods. Smart design can defeat inactivity, boredom, isolation, and depression. With everything so close at hand, and with such a variety of interests and platforms encouraging exploration and well-being, success is just a step outside the front door.

Rincon del Rio's design is as comprehensive and village-like as possible, embracing lifelong learning with younger people and older adults learning computer skills, cooking, sports, and other social activities for seniors.

**FACING PAGE:**
Rincon del Rio has done extensive environmental impact research to ensure that its creation embodies growth and sustainability on all levels, and to avoid encroaching upon the natural beauty that surrounds it.

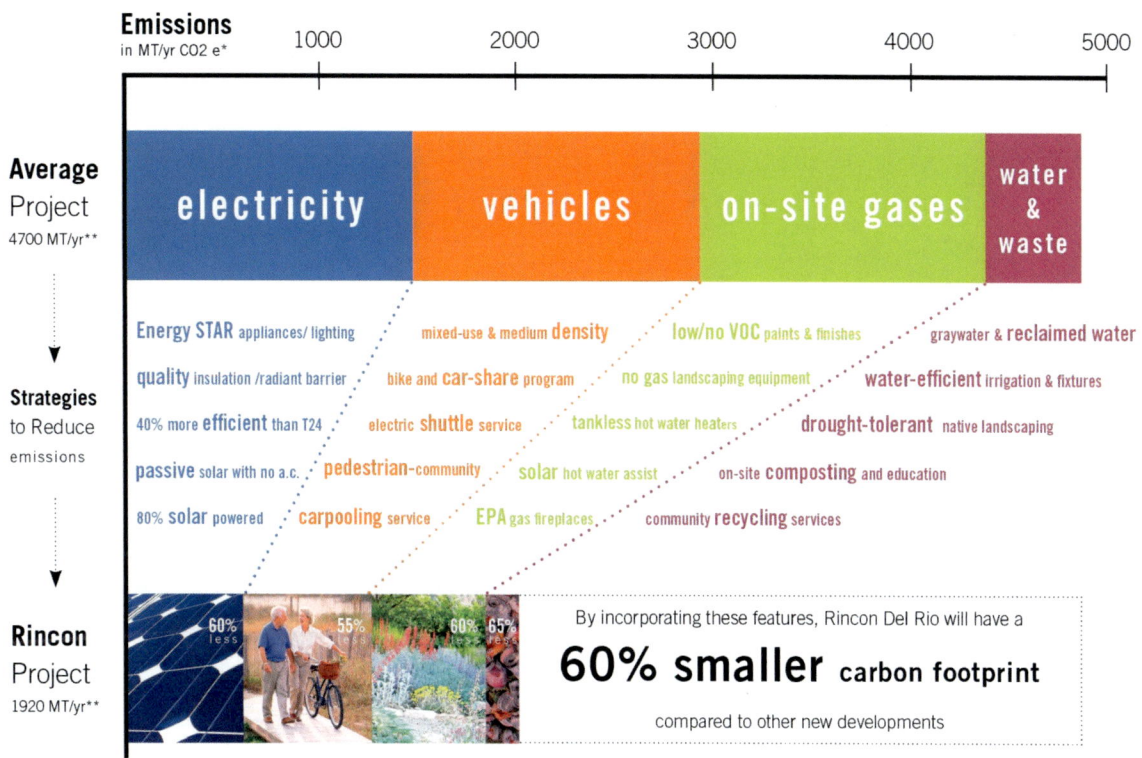

**FACING PAGE:**

The heart of the community is the Village Center, a 90,000-square-foot mixed-use neighborhood where residents and visitors of all ages will congregate. Facing the central plaza are shops, including a bakery, restaurant, sports bar/grill, sundry shop, hardware store, hair and beauty salon, and professional offices, as well as a rose garden, bandstand, kids' area, and other features that elders, adult children, and grandchildren alike will enjoy.

Residences in the Village Center are independent living units, ranging from smaller one bedroom units to larger two bed, two bath units.

**SAME PAGE:**

Rincon del Rio borders the Bear River in southern Nevada County. This river is home to a variety of wildlife, including deer, river otter, several varieties of bird, and fish. It is enjoyed by nature enthusiasts of all ages.

Photo Credit: www.AmericanRivers.org

Since 1880 there haven't been any towns built in Nevada County, California. All of the newer buildings since then have been a sprawl of mini ranchettes or, the new trend, ranchettes without the ranching or big box commercial—but no new towns. Its three existing quaint towns—Nevada City, Grass Valley, and Truckee—are vibrant communities.

**SAME PAGE, TOP:**

Rincon del Rio will be a new village that is inspired by the timeless qualities of small towns like these in Nevada County.

**BOTTOM:**

Front porches invite passersby to say hi, maybe even stop for a cup of coffee. Spontaneous interactions are a natural part of life for residents of a senior cohousing community.

**FACING PAGE:**

Homes are clustered in neighborhoods along rural lanes and shared green spaces, keeping nature and neighbors close at hand.

# American Canyon, California
# Valley View Senior Homes

Valley View Senior Homes is affordable senior housing, inspired by cohousing and the concept that humanity will take care of seniors who might otherwise be homeless. There will be more legacy cohousing projects like this one—projects inspired by cohousing—in the U.S. and Canada than actual cohousing projects. Valley View in American Canyon, California, is such a project.

This project is owned and managed by Satellite Affordable Housing Associates (SAHA), an enlightened not-for-profit developer that believes in community first. Valley View features small homes with small courtyards, all things human scale, all things as connected to the earth as possible. Its very design facilitates people knowing one another and developing positive relationships with one another.

Valley View Senior Homes is influenced by a 1938 collection of articles by John Steinbeck called "The Harvest Gypsies." In these articles, Steinbeck shared the

**FACING PAGE:**
Cottages surround courtyards and pergolas along walkways to the gardens, to the common house, and to public transportation stops. Residents will pass by their neighbors and common facilities during their daily life. These informal interactions promote connection and community. This project was possible because the city set aside a site for seniors who desperately need affordable housing.

**BELOW:**
For the long-term success of a project, it must feel like a place that people are proud of and will want to take care of.

Senior Cohousing Primer—Recent Examples + New Projects

story of cottages and agricultural towns spanning from the Northern Californian town of Redding to San Diego in Southern California. Steinbeck observed how powerful social bonds help individuals persevere through adversity. In this spirit, Valley View Senior Homes is designed to get seniors talking to each other and knowing each other, so they can do a lot for themselves by helping each other.

SAHA hired MDA to help the future residents organize, post move-in. The process is surprisingly straightforward. We start by introducing ourselves to each resident and cooking a common dinner for them. In our line of work, we are often met with resistance until we can prove ourselves to the residents—show them that we understand. We have found that serving a home-cooked dinner is the best platform for a community-building workshop. Everyone likes good food! But more important, the residents grow to understand what it means to be part of a community, and they begin to appreciate their role in it. They learn how to participate in group

**FACING PAGE AND BELOW:**

Seventy affordable rental cottages sit where thirty-five oversized tract houses were once planned. Small houses in clusters on small lanes are reminiscent of villages the world round. With a 53-foot elevation drop from south to north, this site feels more like a southern European hill town than a suburban subdivision.

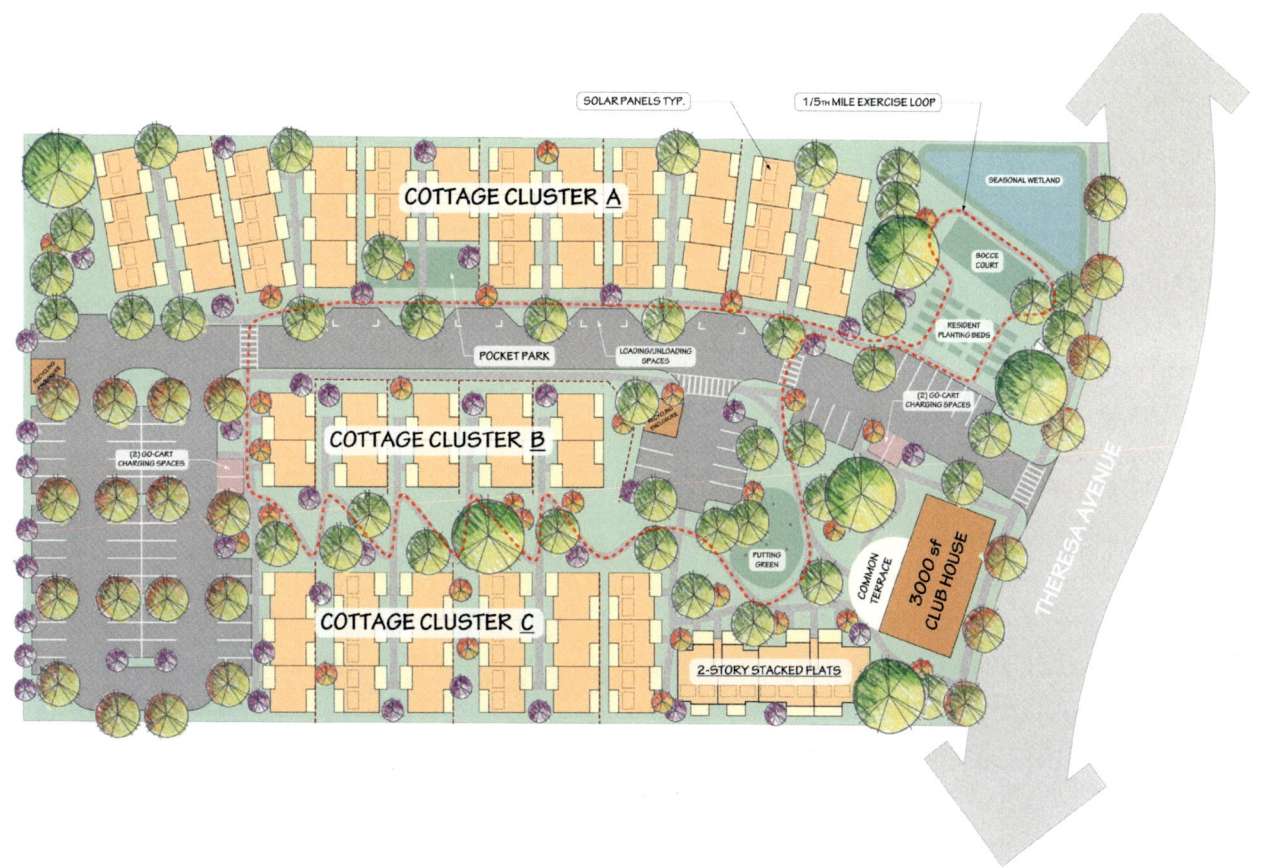

discussion and activities that make their individual lives safer and more enjoyable, not to mention more convenient.

You must appreciate the city of American Canyon, in particular, the head of community development, Brent Cooper, for seeing that "community first" is even more important than "housing first." Valley View Senior Homes is reminiscent of affordable senior housing projects built in Denmark since 1972, when the first Danish cohousing community was completed. Since then, senior housing in Denmark has become a participatory process, utilizing focus groups and smart design with a front porch, pedestrian-oriented atmosphere, where people connect. Residents there participate in community-building workshops, even after moving in. It is a process that instills a self-sustaining social setting where people watch out for and support one another.

Per the Housing and Urban Development (HUD) 2015 statistics, there are about 3.5 million homeless people in America. At about one percent of the country's population, it's a number too big to ignore. Although Valley View Senior Homes is officially low-income senior housing, homeless veterans and others in similar situations can take advantage of projects like these. These small, economical housing developments are in critical demand across the country.

It's important to note that the residents were not involved in the planning of this project, but the project did not progress any faster because of this. It took 10 years, start to finish, to complete Valley View Senior Homes. By contrast, a well-facilitated cohousing project typically takes about two to three years to complete. Simply, a group of future residents generates an urgency, and because they have a personal stake in the outcome they are motivated to move the project along quickly.

> **FACING PAGE:**
>
> Courtyards are connected by walkways and vegetable gardens. Valley View Senior Homes is designed to help seniors successfully age in place. Small cottage scenarios like this one can, and should, be created in towns country-wide.

# Nevada City, California
## Opportunity Village

About a third of the homeless population in the United States is over the age of fifty. Can the cohousing concept provide a solution to homeless seniors? If done in a way that fosters community, the answer is yes.

Opportunity Village Nevada City is inspired by Andrew Heben's book, <u>Tent City Urbanism</u>. The book offers a look at self-organized tent cities across the U.S. in cities such as Ann Arbor, Michigan, and Portland, Oregon, where residents are empowered to change for the better. The tenets of Opportunity Village ring strong in these towns, where city officials and advocates working to end homelessness have their fingers to the pulse of the larger community. The Opportunity Village movement is gaining momentum, especially in places where homelessness is a chronic problem. The leaders in this movement recognize that, first and foremost, homeless individuals want to feel connected to a larger community. Providing a community where these individuals have a voice is the first

**FACING PAGE, CLOCKWISE FROM TOP LEFT:**
Cute little tiny houses on trailers—short-term leases (from the city, the county, or from private property owners) can be put in place to help people in need. Tiny homes like these can help cities and towns effectively accommodate low-income seniors.

Proposed site design for Opportunity Village Nevada City. This intentional design invites residents to converse with each other as they walk to and from the common space and their private homes.

Common walkways lead to the common facilities, which include amenities like a meeting area, kitchen, dining area, and bathroom.

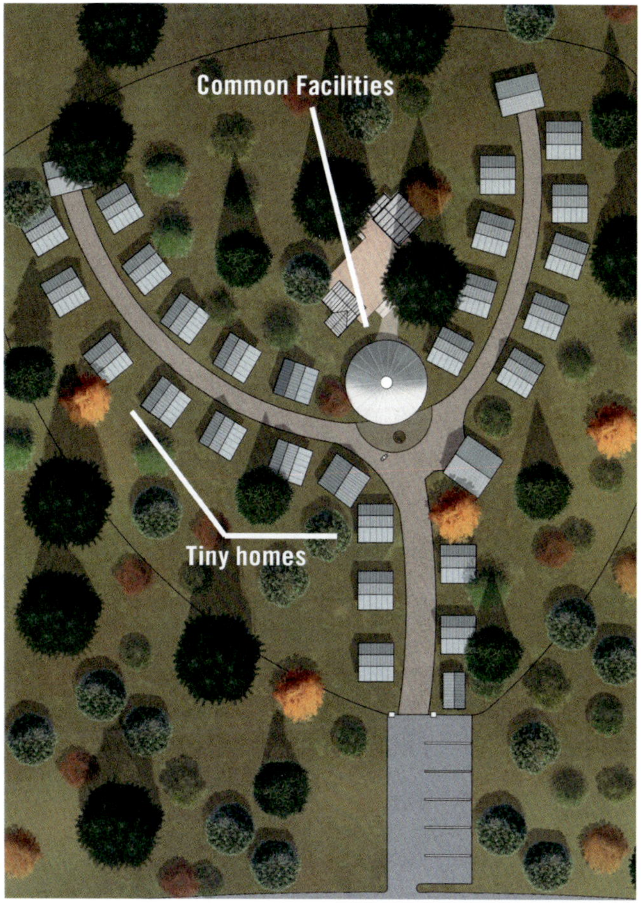

Senior Cohousing Primer—Recent Examples + New Projects   150

step to keeping them off the street and helping them get back on their feet.

Opportunity Village Nevada City will be the first of its kind in Nevada County, California. Currently there are plans to lease one acre of open space. Inexpensive tiny homes will be built on this site, and they will surround a larger community center. The community center will provide showers, toilets, laundry, and a common kitchen. With the support of the county's board of supervisors, the police department, and the larger community, the homeless in Nevada County will have an opportunity to make a fresh start, as has happened at other Opportunity Villages across the country. The tiny houses of Opportunity Village Nevada City will keep people safe and dry while the common facilities provide these otherwise homeless people a way to make dinner for themselves, with each other—for each other. They will have an address, somewhere to call home, and access to a computer and telephone. Here they will build the kind of community and connections that have been proven to pull people out of hopeless situations. Most people are empowered to get out of hopeless situations by family and friends, but not everyone has that support system.

Opportunity Village aims to be a solution to homelessness in Nevada City and its surroundings. The village will provide and foster a most basic need, to be sheltered in a caring community. When built, it will be a safe and secure place where members can support each other and help themselves back to self-sufficiency.

**FACING PAGE:**

These are real people just like you and me. They are ready to make a change in their life. They need a hand up, not a handout. Support their transition and the community will benefit tenfold. Nonprofits can get involved and several have contributed to making Opportunity Village Nevada City a reality. Contact us today to learn how you can become involved. Email info@cohousingco.com.

Senior Cohousing Primer—Recent Examples + New Projects **152**

The residents of Opportunity Village Nevada City will use this community to move themselves up the ladder.

Many homeless folks are extremely capable, and many are capable in limited ways. However, by sharing resources and knowledge a functioning community emerges. Maybe one person knows how to use the bus system, another knows how to shop, and a third knows how to cook. The point is that people intrinsically like to share their know-how, and when people share they help each other.

Left unchecked, homelessness strains municipal resources and public patience. Firefighters and ambulance crews who must travel all about town and into the woods to assist a dispersed population of homeless can put these services out of commission for hours. Unsightly and unwanted loitering near a soup kitchen can make an area feel unclean and unsafe. To be sure, handout services, like soup kitchens, are a needed short-term fix. But long-term we need a setting where a hand up—not a handout—is the norm.

Opportunity Village, complete with tiny houses clustered tightly around common facilities, can easily accommodate county services in one place. This solution could save a community $20,000 to $40,000 per homeless person per year (as reported in towns with similar initiatives). An Opportunity Village also serves as a focal point that brings the broader community together through volunteerism. In a very real sense, helping to build a home for someone without a home creates significant goodwill.

What makes Opportunity Village unique from shelters is that all residents are required to participate in self-governed community meetings. Residents are responsible for general upkeep and maintaining an alcohol- and drug-free environment. These become self-policing communities once the preliminary rules are clearly established and understood. When residents take on more responsibilities, the management volunteers step down, eventually becoming a small or even nonexistent component of village life. Across the country, Opportunity Villages have successfully pulled this off, proving that this solution to homelessness is among the best yet devised.

SAGE Cohousing International is a 501(c)3 nonprofit organization whose vision is to provide resources, training, and guidance, to seniors who want to live in supportive and healthy communities. SAGE Cohousing International works with affordable senior housing projects, such as Opportunity Village Nevada City, as well as other community-oriented housing groups, both cohousing and cohousing-inspired, in the United States.

SAGE Cohousing International aims to make positive social change within the current senior housing market by supporting a community-first approach. In this model, older adults take an active role in their aging scenario, surrounding themselves with neighbors and friends who listen to and care for each other. These groups often go on to co-design and, eventually, co-manage their own senior cohousing neighborhoods. Living in a high-functioning community has proven to mitigate loneliness and depression, improving health and overall being more effectively than other senior housing models.

Become a sponsor today and be a part of the solution in housing for older adults. For more information and to make a donation, visit: SAGECohousingInternational.org.

## Acknowledgements

I'd like to thank my many trusted advisors, the people who encourage me to reach for the ends of the earth in pursuit of my purpose.

Katie McCamant, my collaborator in many projects, continues to be my rock. It is hard to imagine that decades have passed since our first meeting on the streets of Copenhagen, Denmark.

Bill Thomas, doctor, author, and activist for aging successfully, reminds me often to marry the sun and the clouds in my writing and presentations. In his words, senior cohousing is a positive aging scenario, going above and beyond simply mitigating the negative.

My daughter, Jessie, continues to impress me with her growth. She guides my work and my play, and certainly contributes to any impact I may have on the world.

I couldn't have bitten this project off without my sidekick, fellow architect, and author Jean Nilsson, and MDA Culture Worker, Lindy Sexton, who together kept this project on task and moving forward. And, of course, it wouldn't be more than a scribble of thoughts without the generosity of Diane Durrett and Mike van Mantgem—thank you.

Last but far from least, this book would be less than a glimmer in my eye had it not been for the hard working and inspired cohousers that I see every day. Whether it is the folks I live with in Nevada City Cohousing or the senior cohousing groups we work with across the country, these people embrace the benefits (potential and real) of living in community. I've seen it work and am motivated to make senior cohousing a solution for everyone. They need it. We need it.

Thanks, Chuck

## About the Authors

**CHARLES DURRETT** is an architect, author, and advocate of affordable, socially responsible and sustainable design, who has made major contributions to community-based architecture and cohousing.

His firm, McCamant & Durrett Architects, has designed or co-designed more than fifty cohousing communities in the United States, Canada, and New Zealand, as well as projects in Japan and Denmark. The firm's work has been featured in *Time*, *Architecture*, and *The Economist* magazines; the *New York Times* and the *Wall Street Journal* newspapers; and a wide variety of other publications.

Durrett's books include The Senior Cohousing Handbook: A Community Approach to Independent Living (2009, New Society Press); Senior Cohousing Study Group 1 Aging Successfully: Workshop Facilitator Guide and companion Participant Guide (2013, co-authored with Jean Nilsson); and a series of monographs on cohousing.

Creating Cohousing: Building Sustainable Communities, 2011 (New Society Press), which he co-authored with Kathryn McCamant, expands on their 1988 book Cohousing: A Contemporary Approach to Housing Ourselves, which introduced the Danish concept of cohousing to the United States.

**JEAN NILSSON** is an architect who joined McCamant & Durrett Architects in 2004 and has collaborated on the design of cohousing and senior communities as well as on presentations and publications.

Her commitment to community design began in her architectural studies at MIT and UC Berkeley, and her design work includes affordable housing, adaptive reuse of historic buildings as housing, public housing renovation with tenant participation, homeless services projects, and research and guidelines that address housing in historic urban contexts.

In Galveston, Texas, following Hurricane Ike in 2008, Jean assisted in disaster recovery housing efforts to support poor and senior residents, including her parents, who were displaced from damaged areas where demolition and the complex bureaucracy, politics, and financing of rebuilding threatened long-established historic mixed-use neighborhoods of extended families and supportive neighbors.

Made in the USA
Middletown, DE
01 May 2019